Being in the world of modeling where everything is about appearance, I know all too well how the world places an over-emphasis on what we see on the outside. Girls often resort to self-destructive patterns due to this pressure. *Mission of Mercy* is an outstanding book that unpacks all the reasons behind people's struggles. I highly recommend this book—this is one book everyone should read!

—Niki Taylor
International Supermodel

Nancy Alcorn is a force to be reckoned with. I have watched her ministry for years and have seen countless broken lives transformed and many desperate young girls' hope restored. *Mission of Mercy* is a powerful message of hope and healing—the kind that can be found through freedom in Christ. This book will show you that people don't just wake up one day all messed up...there is a reason people are broken, and if we can get to the root of that reason, they can find hope. I am proud to call Nancy a friend and a sister.

—Dave Ramsey
New York Times Best-Selling Author and
Nationally Syndicated Radio Host

For years I've said that leadership isn't about titles, positions, or flowcharts—that it's about one life influencing another. Nancy Alcorn is a stellar example of this definition, and in *Mission of Mercy* she inspires others to lead this way. This book is filled with wisdom, compelling stories, and real-life insight, and it will leave you with a renewed sense of purpose. If you aspire to become a leader who adds value to the lives of those around you, this is a must-read.

—John C. Maxwell
New York Times Best-Selling Author and Speaker

Mission of Mercy will stir the heart of compassion in you and challenge you to live a life devoted to Christ's cause of helping the hurting.

—JOYCE MEYER
BIBLE TEACHER AND BEST-SELLING AUTHOR

Nancy Alcorn is a good friend of mine, and I have watched her ministry change thousands of lives over the years. She is not afraid to deal with the ugly, tough stuff—including sexual abuse, addictions, cutting, and eating disorders. Nancy knows how to get to the core issues and shine the light in the darkness. I believe *Mission of Mercy* will change your life and then in turn help you change the lives of others. Thank you, Nancy, for allowing God to use you to change my life.

—CECE WINANS
GRAMMY AWARD–WINNING ARTIST

The work and ministry that Nancy Alcorn has done over the years truly demonstrates the servant heart of Jesus in reaching out to those in need. Her life and example challenge each of us to get out of our comfort zones and extend God's mercy, grace, and love to those whom society tends to neglect, forget, and overlook—the "least of these." Through this book I believe you'll gain a renewed focus on what being a disciple of Christ looks like practically and be inspired to bring the kingdom of heaven to the world around you.

—ROBERT MORRIS
SENIOR PASTOR OF GATEWAY CHURCH
BEST-SELLING AUTHOR OF *THE BLESSED LIFE*, *THE GOD I NEVER KNEW*, AND *THE BLESSED CHURCH*

Mission of
MERCY

Mission of
MERCY

Nancy Alcorn

CHARISMA
HOUSE

Cover design by Justin Evans
Design Director: Bill Johnson

Visit the author's website at www.mercyministries.com.

Library of Congress Cataloging-in-Publication Data:
Alcorn, Nancy.
  Mission of mercy / Nancy Alcorn. -- First edition .
      pages cm
  Includes bibliographical references.
  ISBN 978-1-61638-962-8 (trade paper) -- ISBN 978-1-61638-963-5 (e-book)
  1. Alcorn, Nancy. 2. Christian biography--United States.
3. Church work with women. 4. Christianity--Psychology. 5.
Mercy Ministries. I. Title.
  BR1725.A317A3 2013
  362.83'575092--dc23
  [B]
                                        2013006354

First edition

13 14 15 16 17 — 987654321
Printed in the United States of America

I Am a Mercy Girl...

I was lost and stumbling in a darkness that I couldn't understand. There was never anyone to talk to who had a clue about my pain. I felt so small... draped in lies and injustice, and the only feelings that could reach me were those of hopelessness, loneliness, isolation, rejection, and desperation. I had no place to go because I didn't feel I belonged anywhere.

Then one day I walked through Mercy's door, and in God's good time I grew strong within their halls of forgiveness, love, patience, understanding, mercy, and grace. Now I stand tall. I am beautiful, refreshed, redeemed, restored, and ready to go.

You can call on me, you can count on me, and you can come to me in your need, just as Mercy came to me in mine. If you want to know what I like most about me...

I am a Mercy Girl...

Acknowledgments

This book would not have been possible without the help of a great team of people who caused all of the elements to come together. I want to extend my personal thanks to the following:

Michele Pillar—no doubt that your part in this book was a divine appointment and sent straight from heaven. This book would have never happened without your invaluable input, creativity, and personal support. Thanks for pushing me to share the painful details and for the countless number of hours we spent together to complete this project.

Ken Mansfield—for being a second pair of eyes in the writing of this book. Your input and creativity were outstanding. God gave me the best!

Janene MacIvor—for your expertise and speed in the editing process. Your flexibility made the difference in us meeting our deadline. You rock!

Ken Abraham—I was blown away that you wanted to read the manuscript and give your feedback. Lucky for me that one of my dearest friends has had multiple number one *New York Times* best sellers!

Debbie Marrie, Charisma House Book Group—for believing in me and the message of this book and for being so great to work with!

Woodley Auguste, Leigh DeVore, and all those at Charisma House Book Group who worked to create such an excellent book.

Acknowledgments

This book would not have been possible without the help of a great team of people who caused all of the elements to come together. I want to extend my personal thanks to the following:

Michele Pillar—no doubt that your part in this book was a divine appointment and sent straight from heaven. This book would have never happened without your invaluable input, creativity, and personal support. Thanks for pushing me to share the painful details and for the countless number of hours we spent together to complete this project.

Ken Mansfield—for being a second pair of eyes in the writing of this book. Your input and creativity were outstanding. God gave me the best!

Janene MacIvor—for your expertise and speed in the editing process. Your flexibility made the difference in us meeting our deadline. You rock!

Ken Abraham—I was blown away that you wanted to read the manuscript and give your feedback. Lucky for me that one of my dearest friends has had multiple number one *New York Times* best sellers!

Debbie Marrie, Charisma House Book Group—for believing in me and the message of this book and for being so great to work with!

Woodley Auguste, Leigh DeVore, and all those at Charisma House Book Group who worked to create such an excellent book.

Michael Briggs—for being a friend to Mercy and connecting us with our publisher.

Katelyn Hamby—for your willingness to read, reread, edit, make suggestions, and the countless hours you spent being such an amazing team player while continuing your normal workload at Mercy.

Reid Cifrino—for being amazingly flexible and for going the extra mile on so many days.

Christy Singleton—for your leadership at Mercy and support of me and the vision of this book.

Elizabeth Williams—for your creative ideas and suggestions. So glad you are a part of our Mercy team!

Rebecca Anderson, my sister—for your help in recalling events from the past and for the extra workload you carried at Mercy during the writing of this book.

Dr. Jane Hamon—for your willingness to make sure my writing lines up with Scripture. You are a wonderful friend!

Margaret Phillips—for allowing me to give our readers an inside look at the seven years of counseling we spent together. I would not be where I am today without you! Thanks also for your help with chapter five.

And last but not least, a very special thanks to the **Mercy graduates** for having the courage to share your stories so that others know that they can experience the same freedom you have experienced.

CONTENTS

Chapter One   Shifting Shadows 1

Chapter Two   Patterns 11

Chapter Three   Broken Places 19

Chapter Four   Stolen Voices 37

Chapter Five   The Great Exchange 55

Chapter Six   White Stones 75

Chapter Seven   The Third Option 91

Chapter Eight   Heart of the Matter 109

Chapter Nine   Fallen Towers 119

Chapter Ten   Choosing Forever 137

Chapter Eleven   Shelters 145

Chapter Twelve   The *Why* Behind the *What* 163

Appendix   More to the Story 171

Notes   211

This book is dedicated to my sister
Beverly Alcorn

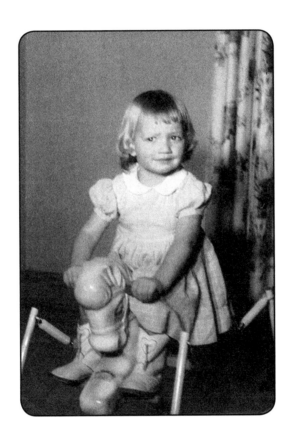

March 1, 1959–May 22, 1962

CHAPTER ONE

Shifting Shadows

THE *PLING, PLING, pling* of my basketball bouncing on the cement court rang though the afternoon air.

To the naked eye I looked like a butter-blonde, eight-year-old shrimp shooting hoops. But in my mind I was Clyde Lee, the six-foot-nine, All-American center for Vanderbilt University, sinking a Hail Mary to win the game right at the buzzer.

Five, four, three, two, one. Swoooosh! Game winner! And the crowd went wild! (Just like my imagination.) I laughed until I thought I'd cry.

I loved pretending to be Clyde Lee under the beautiful blue Tennessee sky. I knew that one day I'd be an all-star player, just like Clyde. I just knew it.

I think this is when I figured out you can't waste time concentrating on what you don't have. Your hopes have to outweigh your obstacles. So I worked on my long shot every day after lunch at New Union Grade School and hated that doggone school bell!

Right on time...there went the bell calling us back to class, and even though I despised it, I didn't fight it. I tossed my ball into the ball box and went inside. I'd just flipped open my notebook and grabbed a freshly sharpened number-two pencil when Principal Freeze's assistant walked into my classroom and straight over to Miss Bartholomew. "Miss B," as we called her, was a tall, genteel soul who made learning fun. I liked having her as my third-grade teacher. School would soon be out for the summer, and I was really going to miss her. Mr. Lamb would be my fourth-grade teacher next year. He was anything but genteel, and nothing like a lamb.

Principal Freeze's assistant walked past the chalkboard looking mad or sad or something. I couldn't put my finger on it, but my guess was that someone was in big trouble. She leaned down and whispered into Miss B's ear, and from my desk on the front row I could tell something was wrong.

Miss B glanced at me and then quickly looked away trying to avoid eye contact. She swallowed hard, and it looked as though her mouth was getting dry as she absorbed what was being said to her. When she motioned for me to come to her desk, I thought I saw her hand trembling a little.

A knot formed in my gut. I got up and walked forward. Principal Freeze's assistant knelt down in front of me. "Nancy, I need you to go straight to the office, honey. OK? Don't dillydally. Go as quick as you can."

"OK, ma'am," I replied.

She opened the heavy classroom door for me and went left as I turned right. "Oh, what have I done?" I asked myself, and tried to imagine what it might be.

As I entered the U-shaped courtyard, my siblings' classroom doors opened almost in unison, and out walked my brother, Bob, and my sisters Dorothy, Rebecca, and Barbara. My sister Susie wasn't born yet.

My knees nearly buckled, and I thought I might throw up but didn't know why. I breathed in and out and swallowed hard to try and make the feeling go away—now *my* mouth was dry. Then I remembered that just thirty minutes ago when I was out on the playground, I heard sirens screaming through the Manchester countryside. The sound of sirens was rare in our sleepy farm town. When they rang out, it was usually something serious, very serious.

As if in a death march I walked down the hall, with my siblings following closely behind me.

When we all got to the office, they sat us down along the gray-green wall like five peas in a pod. Each of us was secretly hoping we were there to get a swat from Principal Freeze for something horrible we had done. That would've been a relief compared to the unknown we were now facing.

The receptionist kept her nose buried in her work. My brother chimed in with the obvious question, "What's going on? Why are we here?"

She looked up from her work and said, "Your aunt will talk to you when she gets here."

Bob would have pushed it, but the lady was flooded with a stream of phone calls. Her switchboard lit up like a Christmas tree.

The minutes passed like hours.

"Do you think it's Mama?" Rebecca asked.

"No," Bob answered. "I think something's happened to Daddy."

I said nothing, but I hoped it wasn't Beverly.

Like a flashback from an old-time movie, my mind replayed the previous night's activities. The very last thing I'd said to Beverly, my three-year-old sister, was, "Leave me alone, or I'll knock your puny head off with this basketball! Go play somewhere else, you little brat! You're nothing but a punk, ya know that?" Beverly hung her head and shuffled away in her little white cowboy boots. She ran into the house and slammed the screen door behind her. When I came in, I got in trouble for what I said to her. Later, when I walked past Beverly's bedroom door, I heard her crying herself to sleep.

It happened the same way almost every night after dinner, and last night was no exception. Like clockwork, Beverly showed up to make my life miserable while I was shooting hoops. And, like clockwork, I returned the favor.

The *pling, pling, plinging* of my basketball bouncing on the cement driveway drew Beverly to me like a bee to honey. And the *click, click, clicking* of her little cowboy boots trampled on my every nerve. She just wanted to be around her big sister. But all *I* wanted was to be Clyde Lee. Her circling right under the basket made it impossible for me to concentrate on my next shot, and I knew I'd be in big trouble if Beverly got hurt with the basketball.

And now, as I sat in the school office waiting for who knew what, I wondered if I'd ever have the chance to say "I'm sorry" to my little sister. I told myself that if she were all right, I'd never, ever get on her case again for pestering me.

Aunt Audra pulled up in front of the school, and we all piled into the car. Still, no one said a word about what was going on. The air in the car was thick as mud, and we knew better than to ask. My aunt pulled into our neighbor's drive and turned off the car.

"Why can't we go home?" I protested.

My aunt didn't answer me. She threw me a look as if to say, "You don't want to know, Nancy."

We were ushered inside and sat down on the couch. Bob suddenly jumped up and looked out the front window at our house. I jumped up too and stayed glued to Bob, knowing he would likely come to some conclusion first, and I wasn't going to miss hearing it when he did.

Bob and I watched as car after car pulled in to our driveway.

"That's it! We're going home!" I insisted.

Our neighbor asked us to stay put, but we ignored her. We walked out the door and headed home, taking long purposeful strides. I'd had enough. We'd all had enough. We wanted to know what the heck was going on.

When my siblings and I walked through our front door, our house was buzzing with relatives cleaning, cooking, and even vacuuming the carpet. It was like Grand Central Station in there. Every aunt and uncle we ever knew was moving around the house in manic motion. It all felt more than a little odd.

My brother looked Aunt Audra squarely in the face and said, "All we've been told is that there was an accident. Is Beverly dead?"

She stared back at my big brother and said nothing. Instead, she barely nodded her head up and down, really slowly, as if answering this way would make it easier for him to take the news.

I was standing behind my brother, peering around him at my aunt when her face told me I'd just lost my little sister. Something deep inside me snapped. My body began walking out the front door, to who knows where.

My friend, the tall, tall oak that stood strong and fast in our front yard, beckoned me to come. I sat beneath his branches and leaned on him for comfort as I had many times before, and I thought about Beverly.

I knew all along it was Beverly the sirens had come for earlier, and I knew all along they weren't able to save her. If she were still alive, or even badly hurt, Mama and Daddy would still be at Coffee County General Hospital holding a vigil and tending to my little sister. We all would be. But we were here, and she was not. And where was Beverly now? *That*, I didn't know. And *that* was the emptiest feeling in the world.

What I *did* know was that I'd never again have the chance to shoo her away from my all-important basketball shots. I'd never again hear the incessant clicking of her boots around my feet, and I'd never get to tell her "I'm sorry."

I'd been sitting there for what seemed like days, but was probably just a few minutes, when an ambulance pulled up in front of me and out stepped my mama and daddy. Mama was crying so loud I'm certain she could be heard in the next county. The attendant helped Daddy up the porch steps and inside the house. Daddy was bent over at the waist, holding his ribs.

Both Daddy and Mama were covered in blood.

A second shock wave went through me. I couldn't move a muscle. I didn't want to go inside and see my grief-stricken parents drenched in my little sister's blood. So I sat under the oak until the sun went down. I don't even remember walking back inside.

My mom's youngest sister sat with us kids on Rebecca's bed and told us about the gruesome tragedy. The tractor got stuck, and my dad asked my mom to pull it out with the farm truck, but because of the mud from last night's rain, the tires slipped. The brakes went out, causing the tractor and truck to jackknife. As usual, Beverly was sitting on my dad's lap on the tractor, and when it all went wrong, her little body was crushed between the steering wheel and his chest. The force of it broke all his ribs.

I'm sure my father felt every bone in Beverly's small body break just as his ribs were breaking—along with his heart.

Her blood covered my dad. While waiting for help to arrive, my parents did all they could to save her, but Beverly died on the way to the hospital.

We sat as still as stones, taking it all in and trying not to cry.

My aunt explained that the doctors had insisted on admitting Daddy to the hospital for traction because of his rib injuries, but he simply refused to stay.

That night, and for many, many weeks, Daddy sat in his chair, rocking back and forth, crying and holding his sides, moaning Beverly's name over and over and over again.

The next morning the house felt all sideways. Nothing felt right side up, and it never would again.

That afternoon a hearse pulled up to the house, and Beverly's tiny casket was carried inside. They placed it on a table near the living room window and propped open the lid. I stood on my tiptoes to see over the side and gazed at what was left of Beverly.

The funeral director carried in a plastic bag containing Beverly's belongings. Her little white boots were in that bag—only now they were splattered with dark red.

As a family, we did the best we could to live beyond Beverly's death, but things were never really the same. We didn't just lose Beverly. We lost Daddy and Mama. We lost our feeling of family. We lost the ability to express any real emotion.

Daddy's eyes glazed over with grief. Even though grandchildren would later bring him joy, his eyes never sparkled again.

Well, almost never again. The day before his passing in 2001, as he lay in Coffee County General, his eyes opened to see God's glory. Even though so close to heaven's gate and struggling for every breath, he found the strength to smile with his eyes—something he hadn't done since the day Beverly left us. My sister Rebecca saw it too. His eyes gleamed all day long as he stared at the top left corner of the room. Rebecca and I agreed he must be seeing Beverly—or angels or both—because it was the same twinkle in his eyes he'd always had when they were together.

I was given the opportunity to speak at Daddy's funeral service, but that was impossible. I couldn't even breathe during the service, let alone talk. But as I sat on the front row, sobbing and fighting my emotions, God gave me a gift. As Uncle Bobby was delivering my father's eulogy, my mind became like a movie screen, and in living color I saw Daddy on his tractor with Beverly in his lap. She, of course, was wearing her little white cowboy boots, and they were both laughing with their heads thrown back in pure joy!

Daddy drove that tractor in huge swooping circles all around that field. It was the most beautiful, free, loving picture of new life—life everlasting—I could have ever asked for. It was a picture of total healing painted for me by the master painter. I knew it was from God because I wasn't in the state of mind to muster such a heavenly vision.

Since then, I never think of Daddy or Beverly without seeing them in this light. After so many years of sadness, only God's handiwork could replace such loss with such life…eternal life.

What *was* is gone. What *is*, is forever, with no tears and no shifting of shadows. What remained with me after that day was a glimmer of hope that I could trust God with my fear of loss—with the shock of loss.

I still had a long way to go before this spark of hope would ignite freedom.

Chapter Two

Patterns

Losing my sister that May afternoon was the first of many untimely losses to plague my life over the next sixteen years. Less than two years after Beverly's death we lost two dear family friends. They lived nearby, and our families were always together. All four parents were best friends. This time it wasn't the screeching of sirens but the ringing of a telephone that was the harbinger of heartrending news. The telephone rang and we received the news of a tragic car accident—the mother and eldest son had been killed.

Then in 1966, less than a year later, it was our pastor and his wife who were taken. They were a young couple I had grown very close to after losing Beverly. I was just starting to open up to them about my grief, something I hadn't yet done with anyone. Now they were gone too as the result of another tragic car crash. That call came in the middle of the night, and from that moment on I could never hear a phone ring at night without breaking into a cold sweat. Our phone was in the hallway, near my bedroom. I hated that phone.

My boyfriend, Andy, abruptly left me the summer after we graduated from high school. We were both planning to go off to college in 1972. He had a full football scholarship waiting for him at the University of Michigan. We'd been hanging out one evening, and after he dropped me off, he went out drinking with his buddies. The phone rang early the next morning with the dreadful news that Andy's car had barreled off a bridge and that he was killed instantly as the result of a broken neck. I loved Andy. I wasn't ready to marry him, but I loved him. He was a fun guy, and we laughed a lot. As I gazed into his casket, I wondered what would have become of him, of us. That was the first time I remember wondering if God was real. "Where is Andy now, God?" I asked. At each new funeral I attended I relived *all* the other funerals. Dealing with so much death made me wonder what this life was really about.

I asked Jesus to come into my heart on August 9, 1972, when my friend from high school took me to a youth testimony service.

The death that seemed to surround me served to usher in the knowledge that God's Son had died for me and conquered death. And because of Him, I could live past the grave too.

But the pattern of death continued in my life. My friend Blanton, a baseball player, was next. He had been my junior high crush, and I kept running in to him after high school. While I was attending Middle Tennessee State University, we bumped into each other once again. He asked if we could go out sometime to catch up on everything and I was excited. I had never forgotten him. I wanted to get to know him as more than a schoolgirl crush. I winked and warned him that there had been a huge change in my life, referring to Jesus, and he said he'd heard all about it through the grapevine. We both smiled, understanding that he would be getting an earful of the gospel on our date.

That same weekend Blanton went mountain climbing on Monteagle. He was an expert climber but broke the number one rule: *never* climb alone. We got word on Sunday that he was missing. A search party found Blanton's body before the day's end. He had been able to drag himself quite a distance from where he'd fallen, searching for help before his body gave out and he died.

Years later, at my mother's eightieth birthday party, Blanton's mother came by. She pulled me aside and told me that Blanton always said I was the kind of girl he'd want to marry. After so long, it was a bittersweet thing to hear. Blanton had a great heart. He was a good man, and I'm sad we never got to go on that date. I was never able to tell him about my faith in Jesus. I hope Blanton felt God with him on that trail and knew He had come to take him home on that fateful day in 1973. I pray God comforted him before he died.

Two of my first cousins left us in the seventies, one in a car accident and the other in a suicide. In 1978 my beloved brother-in-law Al died instantly in a car crash at the age of twenty-nine, leaving my sister and their two beautiful children behind. Then cancer took one of my aunts, and another cousin died unexpectedly from a brain aneurism.

I felt out of balance, and it was obvious that so much loss and the accompanying fear were the culprits. I couldn't enjoy friendships or dating relationships. I was afraid to get married. I was afraid to connect, period. In addition to those fears, thinking something might happen to anyone who got close to me was torment. That crippling fear was *what* kept me from getting close to people. And my need to wear a permanent "game face" to hide the fear was the *why* that followed. I was the consummate outgoing leader everyone could count on, but inside I was struggling. We all have the need to love and be loved, but my fear of loss was greater, and it was robbing me of both.

I knew I needed help, so I went to the Word of God. I studied. I read books and listened to Bible teachers on how to pray and what God promises us about being free from fear, grief, and torment. I believed there had to be a stronghold in my family bloodline. I was angry and tired of losing people and wanted to know if there was anything I could do about it. God began teaching me to pray with the authority He gives to believers to stop the destructive plans of the enemy. I found Psalm 119:68, which showed me that God *is* good and He *does* good. I also discovered that when we are born again, the powerful blood of the innocent Christ supersedes the bloodlines we were born into. Galatians 3:13 tells us that in Christ the curse is broken.

I began praying God's protection over existing family members and over every baby born into our family. I began telling the enemy he was not permitted to take anyone else through untimely tragedy. At first, praying this way felt awkward because I had grown up being taught that everything that happens is the will of God. But through His Word God was showing me differently.

In the beginning I had no way of knowing if my prayers were making a difference. But it was quiet on the home front, and it wasn't long before I saw clear evidence that my prayers were working.

I was living in Monroe, Louisiana, at the time. The phone rang one evening, and when I heard the concern in my mother's voice, my heart sank. Following is the conversation as I remember it.

"Nancy, today while your sister Dorothy was out running errands she pulled into a car wash," she began. "Little Melissa was in the front seat playing with her dolls. When Dorothy got out of the van to wash the car, a man approached her with a gun and, without a word, aimed it at Dorothy and pulled the trigger, but nothing happened.

"Dorothy ran to find help. People's Bank was nearby, but she slipped on the wet cement and fell to the ground. He aimed at her head and fired again, and still the gun didn't fire. She got up to run, and he fired a third time to no avail.

"She entered the bank, hysterical, telling them about 'a man with a gun,' and they locked all the doors and wouldn't let Dorothy leave. She pleaded with them to set her free for the sake of her three-year-old daughter who was still in the van with the keys in the ignition, but they would not unlock the bank doors no matter what she said.

"She finally convinced them to let her go, and when she got out, here came little Melissa walking up the sidewalk toward the bank, still holding her baby doll and without a hair on her head out of place. Melissa is safe because the man abandoned the van just a block away from the Ready Wash, leaving his gun and Melissa still inside.

"Melissa and Dorothy are just fine, Nancy."

I stood there in amazement as I listened to how God had protected my loved ones. After a moment I said to my mother, "This was God. There's no other logical explanation for it."

Forensic study concluded that there was absolutely no reason for the bullets to remain in the gun. They shot the gun numerous times without failure. Not only did God protect Melissa and Dorothy that day, but He also provided scientific proof to confirm divine intervention is real.

Another time, my sister Barbara was driving on a curvy road, going approximately forty miles per hour. Her young daughter Janet was in the backseat. For no apparent reason, the back door flew open and Janet tumbled out of the car. She walked away from the incident without a scratch.

Some people think it's a coincidence, and some people would say it's because of prayer. But for whatever reason, there have not been any tragedies in our family since the time God began teaching me how to pray this way. And for that I am so thankful. I'm sure God used prayers other than mine to accomplish His work on our behalf, but I'm grateful to have played a part. It served to empower me in my faith and heal me of my fear.

One of our greatest needs is to be *fully* understood and still loved regardless of our issues. God understands us completely and loves us unconditionally, yet He loves us enough to change the way we are when our *why* creates a *what* that keeps us from living freely and abundantly.

Now you know one of my *whys* behind one of my *whats* and how God worked to free me from the fear of loss. I have many more imperfections you'll read about before turning the last page of this book, but God doesn't wait until we are perfect before calling us to make a difference in this world. If you're a person waiting to be something before you can do something, remember He specializes in using imperfect people to do His perfect work.

I am living proof.

CHAPTER THREE

Broken Places

As I write, the sun has risen and set 18,630 times since I lost my sister Beverly. And just as the sun burns strong and bright in the eastern sky each morning, so God's mercies are new each time I open my eyes to a brand-new day. Each day is another chance to get it right, to allow God to work in and through me simultaneously.

In many ways I am completely different from the girl who sat weeping under an old oak in 1962. Who wouldn't be different fifty years later? And yet, truth be told, there's a part of me that still feels eight years old. I often wish I could run back there and find shelter under that old oak tree, a place that now exists only in my memory bank.

Have you ever noticed? We grow and change, and God takes us from glory to glory, yet at times we feel as if we haven't budged an inch along the way. We never really feel ready for life's challenges, tasks, or opportunities when they drop into our laps. And we shouldn't be shocked when we rise to an occasion and are better than we dreamed we ever could be, because the truth is, with God we *are* better than we believe we are.

That was the conflict churning inside me the 1983 winter day I rolled out of my Nashville driveway and headed for Monroe, Louisiana, to open the first Mercy Ministries home for troubled girls. I didn't feel ready. I didn't feel capable.

I had a thousand dollars in my pocket that had been there less than twelve hours. The money was a gift from my friends the night before. And my warhorse was a jalopy, filled to the brim with my meager belongings. But after all I'd seen, after all God had shown me during the past ten years, I knew without a doubt what *didn't* work, and I knew God had tutored me in what *would* work.

My belly burned with a fire to see if we could do this thing called rehab one better. It was time to replace *rehabilitation* with *restoration*. In my mind it wasn't going to be a word game built on empty rhetoric, research statistics, labels, and medications to mask the problems. It was going to be a physical place where the living God could walk and talk and breathe real change into the broken lives of young women.

And it was stamped on my work order from God Himself to do it with the Bible as our manual, the Holy Spirit as our Counselor, and the blood of Jesus as our permission slip. What was there to lose? I'd seen firsthand how the wisdom of man left girls empty—as empty as my other three pockets. The experts had failed every single woman I'd worked with in the eight years I drew a paycheck from the Tennessee State government. Frustration and compassion were my motivators, and witnessing girl after girl return to her same affliction—to her own vomit—upon release from bars and razor wire was what kept my car pointed toward Louisiana.

Since that drive, 11,112 suns have set over that first Mercy home. Its doors have welcomed more than a thousand girls—priceless daughters of God—all willing warriors in this spiritual revolution.

Years later, there are now seven Mercy homes where thousands of young women experience new beginnings in Christ. Each home is equipped with qualified, loving staff members. This has given me the freedom to travel around the world speaking in conferences and churches, sharing the message of God's power to transform lives.

One Easter morning I shared the platform with Pastor Joel Osteen. We spoke to forty-five thousand people at Minute Maid Park, home of the Houston Astros. How generous of Pastor Joel to provide me the opportunity to tell so many people about the *why*s behind the *what*s of Mercy Ministries. I wore a sky-blue suit in honor of our risen Christ, and as I stepped onto that stage, I couldn't help but wonder how on earth I'd gotten there.

I cleared my throat and shouted, "He is risen!," after which I thanked Joel and the entire Osteen family for the opportunity to speak that morning.

I scanned the arena, took in the massive crowd of God's people, and told them my story.

I spent the first five years of my career working in a correctional facility for teenage girls. These young women weren't there because they wanted help. They were sent there by juvenile court judges for committing criminal offenses and were too young to go to the women's prison. My job was athletic director. Every girl was required by law to participate in some type of recreational activity daily.

There were three hundred teenage delinquent girls there at any given time. It was set up just like a women's prison, except they were teens. The guards carried mace. The fences were fifteen feet high and topped with coiled barbed wire infused with razor blades. And if anyone tried to escape, there was a guards' tower to make sure they didn't. If you have ever visited a prison or seen one in a movie, you know what the campus looked like.

I had become a Christian after high school right before I went to college and was still thinking I would become a basketball coach. So I majored in health, physical education, and recreation, and coached part time on the side. But I was drawn toward people who had life-controlling issues. Plus, I was trying to hear from God, asking Him, "What is Your plan for my life? What am I supposed to do with my life?"

I loved sports, and I loved the idea of coaching, but I was also interested in social services, psychology, and criminal justice, so I made them my minors. Little did I know that having these degrees in my pocket would help it all come together. After college I had everything I needed to qualify for working at that government facility for young women.

Even when you think you're confused, you can look back and see that God had His hand on your life. The Word of God says that He orders our steps and He directs our path, and as a Christian I really believe that. I also love Proverbs 3:5–6 because it asks us to trust in the Lord with all our hearts and lean not on our own understanding but acknowledge Him in all our ways, and He *will*—not He might, but He *will*—direct our paths.

Although I was confused about my college coursework, God had His hand on me and He was ordering my steps and directing my path. That first five years of my eight years of government work gave me the heart for what I'm doing with Mercy Ministries today.

At the juvenile facility the girls were ages fourteen to eighteen. During staff orientation they explained that because it was a government-funded facility under the state of Tennessee's jurisdiction, we were not allowed to share anything about the Christian message. My heart sank because I really believed that the same Christ who changed my life could change the girls' lives too.

Learning that I would not have the freedom to talk to those young women about the only One who could forgive their sin, heal their broken lives, and give them a new beginning just as God had done for me was beyond disappointing.

When I talked to the warden about it, she told me she "kind of" knew where I was coming from because she was "kind of" a backslid Christian herself. And if you can imagine, she told me this while smoking a cigarette and blowing the smoke directly into my face. I'm thinking, "Well I kind of like you already because you kind of get me a little bit." And I said, "Well, I'm not really backslid and I'm kind of front slid…I'm excited about being here and I want to make a difference!"

The warden leaned forward and gave me a look that meant business. "Hey, if the girls ask you a question about your faith, you can answer it, but you can't bring up the subject yourself."

"Fair enough," I said and chalked up two points for the kingdom of God.

I would say things to provoke the girls to ask questions, and they did, quite a bit. I tried to go by the rules because I didn't want to lose my job, but I prayed for God to give me opportunities.

The thing that broke my heart the most was that we had "great" experts there, psychiatrists and psychologists. They ran psychological tests and prescribed medication when needed. They told these young women all the reasons why they were the way they were. And the experts told the girls that they were the way they were because of their parents' and grandparents' backgrounds, they would always

24

be this way, and it would be the same for their children. They were giving them nothing but a doom and gloom picture of the future.

As a Christian I knew that Jeremiah 29:11 says, "'I know the plans I have for you,' declares the LORD, 'plans to prosper you and not to harm you, to give you hope and a future'" (NIV). And yet these well-trained, well-meaning experts, many of whom didn't believe in God, ran the tests and told them all the reasons why they would never be able to overcome their current circumstances. The Bible tells us, as a man thinks, so is he. I took every opportunity to reprogram the girls' thinking saying, "There is a way that you can have a new beginning. There is a way that you can be forgiven. There is a way you can have a new start." And I would pray for chances to tell them.

On the plus side I was allowed to show Christian movies because Christians donated the films, such as *The Cross and the Switchblade*, which is about David Wilkerson, the founder of Teen Challenge, an outreach in New York City. The film shows how David worked with drug addicts and prostitutes to lead them to Christ.

Contemporary Christian bands came in from Nashville and did concerts for us. It was allowed because they didn't ask for pay. They had a message they wanted to share, and they cared about that message. They cared about the girls.

And we had all kinds of Christian books donated to us, including some about prostitutes and drug addicts whose lives had been changed. Nicky Cruz wrote a book called *Run Baby Run*. And Cookie Rodriguez was a delivered and restored drug addict and prostitute, whose book we offered the girls. Other such books flooded in because Christians who learned about what was going on in the facility pooled their money and provided resources for us.

I looked up the definition of *recreational activities* in my college textbook. The definition included recreational reading, so that's how I was able to set up a library. The girls would come check out books and we would show movies.

Out of fifty-five staff members, one of them ratted on me—I'm still not sure which one. She complained to the warden that Nancy Alcorn [or *Coach* as they called me], well, all her books are Christian, all her movies are Christian, all her music groups are Christian, so we would like to have some that are *not* Christian!

Soon after the complaint I got called up to the warden's office. (The Bible is cool because it says that if you are ever in a situation where you get caught off guard and you don't know what to say, you just trust that at that very moment God will fill your mouth with whatever it is you need to speak.)

I won't lie to you; I was a little nervous, but I didn't think I had done anything wrong. I prayed and said to God, "OK, God, help me, because I don't know what this is about."

I was ushered into the warden's office by her executive assistant, and the door shut behind me. The warden had on one of those really nice "Bonnie and Clyde" suits—a really straight skirt and a tight jacket—and she was very classy. She leaned back in her chair and lit up one of those Camel cigarettes with no filter. I guess whatever it was that she was going to talk to me about, she felt like she was going to need company. She said, "Nancy, I gotta tell you, we've had some complaints that every music group you bring in, every book you have in the library, and every movie you show is all Christian stuff. Is that true?"

I replied that was true.

The warden said, "Well, we talked about this, you know."

I agreed that we had.

"Can you explain to me what the problem is?"

I took a deep breath. "Here's the problem: all these books and movies are donated, and music groups give of their time because they believe in the message that they are sharing. I'm happy to mix it up, and we can bring secular bands in here, and we can have secular books and we can have secular movies, but you're going to have to give me a budget to do that."

She took a really deep, deep, long drag on that cigarette and blew it all out, looked at me, and said, "OK, I get your point. That will be all."

She let me go. I wasn't in trouble, and she never complained about it again.

God was with me yet another time when two girls jumped out of the stands in the gym one night and started a full-on fistfight over a library book. Imagine a sports event during which two players break out in a fight and both teams jump in to help. This night the bleachers emptied, and all the inmates were running out onto the floor. They were clawing at each other, pulling hair, and after it was all sorted out, I was bleeding too.

All this commotion was over a Christian book. I called my friends and said, "You guys better buy me some more books or these girls are going to kill each other because they really want to read these testimonies!" And you know what God showed me out of that? The reason they were fighting over a little book is because they desperately wanted to believe that *maybe, just maybe, their lives could change too.* One little book gave them big hope. We had more books brought in so they would never have reason to fight over hope again. This definitely got my attention.

I remember looking out over the expanse of the campus one afternoon. There were six huge dorms filled to capacity, flanked by a large cafeteria and a Laundromat. I remember thinking and dreaming, "What would it be like if every single person who worked here believed in God and had firsthand experience in knowing that He can give someone a new heart, a new spirit, and that God heals the broken places in a person's life and sets captives free? And believed He forgives sin, abolishes shame, guilt, and condemnation, even for a prostitute who feels she is dirty and will never be anything, and no one would ever want her because of the choices that she made?"

What we as Christians need to remember is that these young women were shaped by their families and by the parents they were born to. God started showing me how not to judge them. You see, there is always a temptation to judge when we are around people who are acting out in ways we don't agree with and don't understand. God opened my eyes and showed me all the reasons why I shouldn't judge them.

I was having a particularly hard time loving one of the girls, and I said, "God, I recognize that I'm judging this girl, but what am I going to do here? I need help. I know I'm not supposed to feel this way, but there's just something about her that makes me not want to be around her."

I found myself avoiding this girl because I didn't like how she acted, the way she treated other people, and the way she looked. I didn't like anything about her. Doing the good little Christian thing we do sometimes, I put her name on my prayer list, and I started praying for her. And one morning when I was praying, it was like God just said, "*Stop!* You're not praying for her benefit; you're praying for yourself because you feel guilty for not liking her."

God has a way of helping you get real with yourself. I remember crying that day and saying, "God, I don't know how to love her." And He said, "That's all I needed to hear you say. If you will let Me, I'll open your eyes to see her the way I see her and love her the way I love her."

"Well, where do I start?"

And God told me, "Go read her case record."

It was the most horrendous case I had ever read. This girl had been used, abused, raped, abandoned, and beaten. She had been abused—physically, sexually, emotionally—every way you can be abused. And I'm talking *extreme* abuse. It took all my energy to read that file in one sitting because it was that painful.

What I heard in my heart was, "Nancy, if you had been born into that family and you had all those things happen to you, then you would be just like her."

That changed everything for me.

It made me realize that all of us have moments in our lives when we judge people, but we've never really walked where they walked, lived where they lived, or experienced exactly what has happened to them.

God had gotten a hold of my heart in that moment. Then He added, "Remember: There's always a *why* behind the *what*. There's always a reason why people are the way they are. None of these kids decided when they were little girls playing with dolls that they wanted to grow up and live in a correctional facility. That wasn't their plan, and yet here they are."

I recognized out of that experience that there had to be a better way than the way we were doing it. The girls were kept in that facility for a year to supposedly be rehabilitated, yet they would get out and nothing would change. For the girls who had been prostitutes, their pimps were waiting on them. For the girls who had been using drugs, their dealers were waiting on them too and knew exactly when they were getting out. For gang members it was the same thing. Gangs were right there waiting to take the girls back and reengage them in the same illegal activities.

After working with these girls for a year, you could begin to see their potential—you could see gifts, talents, and abilities—and so my frustration mounted. I knew if they had the right opportunities and worked out some things, they could turn their lives around before it was too late. And again, I was frustrated because I couldn't fully tell them about the One who had changed my life.

The girls would go home, and we'd hear about some of them dying from drug overdoses and getting killed in street gang fights. Some even took their own lives before their eighteenth birthdays.

A few years later while working on my master's degree, I was assigned an internship at the Nashville Women's Prison. It was heartbreaking to see some of the young women I had known as teenagers at the juvenile facility now serving hard time in the women's prison, their lives wasting away. It's a "no wonder" these women had become casualties. Who wouldn't have, if experts told you there was no hope for you and that you could never change and that you would always be this way?

That's when I really began to cry out to God and said, "I love my job, but I don't want to spend my whole life working in a system that looks good and sounds good on paper and our taxpayer dollars are paying for it, but the reality is that lives aren't changing." The success rate the government had for rehabilitation—via their own study—showed less than 3 percent.

And that sums up the first five years of my career: seeing the *whys* behind the *whats* in people and what does not work to help them.

I was asked to transfer to the Department of Human Services and take a job in the inner city of Nashville, Tennessee, with the Emergency Child Protective Services Unit. In that unit I was on call twenty-four hours a day and carried a beeper. If that beeper went off, no matter where I was or what I was doing, I had to go in. There were many, many nights when I met the police on emergency calls and saw firsthand little girls and little boys who had been horribly sexually abused by grown men and women who should have been their protectors. There were many little children who had been physically beaten.

One night a mother who was a drug addict and a prostitute left her young son with her boyfriend in a sleazy hotel room downtown. The kid was screaming and the hotel people were going nuts and called the police. When we arrived, the police had to break the door down. The little boy was covered in blood, and a man who was supposed to be babysitting was crouched in the corner. He was holding a shoe that was covered in blood. He had just about beaten the little boy to death with the heel of his shoe.

The officer walked toward the man and I knelt down in front of the little boy. I asked him carefully, "Can you please tell me what happened here tonight, sweetie?"

"Bad man beat me," he said. The child could barely get these words out. It was more groaning than speaking. Tears fell from his little eyes and mixed with the blood on his face.

That child was rushed to the hospital and was in critical condition for hours. He pulled through, but not by much. I still wonder today what happened to that little boy because of the trauma of that night and the obvious lack of nurturing and care he received. All children need care and love. It was just so heartbreaking.

I spent three years investigating child abuse cases and seeing this awful stuff. The sexual abuse was the hardest for me. We had to sit across the table from the perpetrators and gather details for the case records. It was very, very difficult, and I was very conflicted as a Christian. We're supposed to love and care for everybody, but it was almost impossible. I was so angry with the people I had to look at and talk to because of the unthinkable things they had done to a child.

I began to have nightmares. I cried out to God that there had to be a better way. I was a big complainer back then, and said, "God, I'm mad at You. I don't want to do this anymore. I don't like what I'm seeing. Why are You making me look at this?"

I used to be able to hear about abuse like this on the news and read about it in the newspaper and go on about my business. But when I looked into those little children's faces and saw what had happened to them with my own eyes, I could no longer just go on as if nothing had happened. Those images are still with me to this day. I think it is God's design because it continues to motivate me to remember that when someone is bad, there is a reason why—the *why* behind the *what*—there is a reason why they are the way they are, and there is a God who can heal what is broken. He can restore what is stolen, and He can make right what is wrong.

I cried out to God, "What are You doing with me?"

He said, "You just spent five years dealing with angry teenage girls in a correctional facility, and now I'm taking you back in time and showing you why they are so angry."

That was the *why* behind the *what*.

God was trying to teach me not to judge the *who* or the *what*, but that it is of utmost importance to understand the *why* because that is the only way a heart can ever be restored.

John 10:10 says, "The thief does not come except to steal, and to kill, and to destroy. I have come that they may have life, and that they may have it more abundantly.'" And after eight years of working for the government, I began to understand that God has not equipped or anointed the government to heal broken hearts and set captives free.

He has called us, His people, to do it. I needed to be in a place where I had the freedom to share the message that no matter what you've done, you can be forgiven. God will meet you right where you are. He will give you a new heart. He will give you a new spirit. He will give you a new beginning. He didn't cause the abuse, but He will use what happened to you to build a story in you to tell others—a testimony, if you will—to help other people understand that if God can help you, then He can also help them.

God is calling us all to believe what He has told us in James 2:13: mercy always triumphs over judgment, always.

I thanked Joel and Victoria and everyone at Lakewood Church for partnering with Mercy Ministries. I stepped away from the pulpit, and Joel met me halfway across the massive stage. He hugged me and whispered in my ear, "Great job, Nancy!"

Joel is the encourager of all encouragers.

I sat with Joel's mother and family in the front row and heard one of the best Easter sermons of my life. Loving sports the way I do, it was extra cool to me that we were sitting in a packed-out baseball stadium celebrating the resurrection of our Savior, something much greater than winning a World Series.

After the service we shared an Easter brunch at a fine hotel. The Osteens are like an adopted family to me, so it meant so much to be included in this special family time.

It warmed my heart to see Mercy's work playing out as Joel's sister Lisa's twin girls ran around the table. Her husband, Kevin, chased them with their son, Christopher, over his shoulder. It seems like only yesterday when Lisa and Kevin adopted their twin daughters and then two years later adopted their son from courageous birth mothers at Mercy.

Mercy Ministries has been a bridge for me to meet so many wonderful people who share my passion for seeing broken lives restored.

January 2013 marked thirty years since the desire God put in my heart became a reality called Mercy Ministries. I thought I was starting *one* home for troubled young women. I had no idea this would grow to become multiple homes in America, as well as homes in other nations.

Chapter Four

Stolen Voices

WHY WON'T SHE stop crying?" Mike pleaded with his wife, Laura.

"I have no idea, sweetheart," Laura assured him.

But Laura was lying.

Even though just forty-two days into this thing called motherhood, Laura knew exactly why their brand-new baby daughter wouldn't stop crying when Mike held her. This *knowing* came from somewhere deep inside Laura's gut. Women, especially mothers, just know these things, even if they never say them out loud. Even if they can't admit to themselves that they know.

Some call it women's intuition. Christian women often gather this kind of information from the Holy Spirit, but Laura gathered it from personal experience.

When it came to relationships, especially with women, her husband, Mike, gave off a particular vibe, and not a good one. He could say more with one look than Laura could say with a thousand curt words. And he was generous about delivering these looks. Laura had been on the receiving end of his cold, condescending glares too many times to count. He shot them like bullets anytime he wanted to gain ground, feel powerful, or even just to get his own way. He hadn't even had the decency to lay off this cruelty during her pregnancy. Laura fought miscarriage multiple times with this baby, thanks to Mike's verbal and emotional abuse. The doctor spoke with him about it, but he didn't stop.

Laura and Mike were just beginning their second year of marriage when Laura got pregnant with Nichole. While they were dating, Laura was so "in love with being in love" she chose to ignore Mike's male chauvinism. But soon after their honeymoon her eyes saw it all in 20/20. She considered leaving him six months after the wedding, but her Christian upbringing wouldn't let her give up that soon. And now they had a baby. She was stuck.

She prayed—and often—for God to get to Mike. She asked Jesus to "knock him down a few notches" but wasn't sure it was very Christian-like to pray such things. So sometimes she'd change her wording around to sound pretty and polite.

"Maybe that will work better. Maybe God likes good manners," she thought to herself, knowing that God was hearing it the way she prayed it the first time.

What Laura didn't understand was that God heard the intent of her heart, no matter the words she used. God was hearing yet a third prayer coming from a place in Laura that only He could reach, only He could hear, only He could know. He was hearing her cries for a defender, a protector, an advocate for both her and Nichole against this bully—a prayer Laura didn't even know she was praying.

Laura knew the effect Mike's mean spirit had on her. "What will it do to an innocent little girl?" she wondered. This wondering kept Laura up at night.

Mike had spent the last hour trying to put Nichole down for a nap, and, as usual, he gave up and handed Nichole over to Laura. The baby fell fast asleep the moment she felt Laura's touch.

Baby Nichole was afraid of men from the day she came home from the hospital. When Nichole was two, Mike shaved off his beard in hopes it would help, but nothing changed.

From the age of five Nichole tried spending the night with friends but couldn't. By 10:00 p.m. Laura would get a call asking her to come pick up Nichole because she couldn't stop crying. She was too afraid of her friends' fathers.

Nichole's third-grade year, Laura requested a male teacher,

hoping it would cure Nichole of this phobia. But that didn't work either. And now Nichole was in high school, burdened with anorexia and clinical depression. By this time Laura was taking an antidepressant, but nobody except the doctor knew about that, not even Mike.

In her junior year Nichole made the girls basketball team. She loved running the length of the court, hoping to burn off a million calories and to escape her own mental hell. But that ended abruptly when her father pulled her aside after a big game to announce he was disowning her because she hadn't scored enough points and that he blamed her single-handedly for losing the championship game.

After quitting basketball, Nichole tried modeling. Instead of running to burn off calories, she used caffeine and uppers to stay thin. Nichole ended up tearing her head shots into tiny little pieces after her dad said her nose looked too big in one of the photos.

Nichole had nightmares about men doing horrible things to her and woke up in a cold sweat at least once a week. At the same time she clung to every boy she dated and would do anything they wanted as long as they promised to never leave her. She lost her virginity at age fourteen and soon after found that young man in bed with another girl at a party. Instead of breaking up with him, Nichole begged him to stay with her. He stayed, but now he thought he *owned* Nichole and could talk to her however he liked. He continued sleeping around whenever he felt like it. Nichole increased her medication and lost more weight one skipped meal at a time as she continued to lose her self-esteem—an esteem she never had to begin with.

After a feeble attempt at suicide, Nichole landed in a psychiatric ward not far from her house. She was released almost immediately because her dad railed on the administration. He convinced them that Nichole was getting the help she needed at their home church and at school, although he never attended church.

Against their better judgment, her doctor and treatment team agreed to Nichole's release with the condition that they receive regular reports from her high school counselor. The high school counselor agreed and provided reports to Nichole's parents, who then sent them in. Mike turned the reports in right on time, but not before falsifying them. Laura didn't know about Mike's deception. Mike told Nichole that her stint in the hospital was a bad reflection on both him and the family. Nichole plummeted into an even deeper depression.

"You better shape up, missy!" was how Mike put it to Nichole, so she became a very convincing actress. Mike was too blinded by his ego to see through her performances.

After high school Nichole left home and entered beauty school. For eight long months she cried herself to sleep and was pulling Cs and Ds on her test scores. She was miserable and had to move back in with her parents. She graduated from beauty school—barely scraping by—and again moved out of her parents' house. She moved in with a new boyfriend and slept holding onto him tightly every night. Three months into the relationship, she found out he was having sex with someone else and, just like before, she put up with it. He told Nichole she was too "high maintenance" and that sleeping around was the only way he knew how to cope with her.

Desperate, Nichole tagged along with a friend to a church youth meeting hoping to find something, anything, to help her keep her boyfriend and stave off thoughts of suicide.

There she met the senior pastor, Jim, and his wife, Carla. Jim was a kindhearted, loving man who took Nichole under his wing. For the very first time in her life Nichole found a father figure as well as safety, security, and freedom from her fear of men.

After getting to know Nichole a little better, Pastor Jim encouraged her to come in for counseling appointments. After talking and praying with him for a few weeks, Nichole found the strength to ask her boyfriend to move out of their apartment. She lived alone and was at peace for the first time in her life.

One afternoon Pastor Jim and Carla stopped by Nichole's apartment with a basket of homemade muffins and a bouquet of wild flowers, Nichole's favorite. They told her how proud they were of her progress and encouraged Nichole to keep pressing in to God.

Later that day Pastor Jim swung back by to pick up the cell phone he'd left behind earlier. He stayed for a while, and they talked at length about her dad and her need to experience unconditional love. That did it. When they held hands to pray together, they embraced, and without missing a beat he kissed her. By the next afternoon they were in bed together, and Nichole wasn't quite sure how it all happened.

Jim and Nichole were intimate for months. Nichole stopped

going to church so she wouldn't have to fake it around everyone. She loved Jim, or so she thought. Her feelings ran deep but were not without God's conviction. She called Jim and told him she missed her friends at church and was feeling guilty and alienated from God but was hoping he'd keep his promise to marry her one day. This struck panic in Jim's heart, and he told Nichole that if she breathed a word to anyone, he'd deny the entire affair.

"They'll never believe you in a million years, Nichole," he said, and hung up.

The next evening Jim called Nichole and broke it off altogether, telling her to never call him again. He added to her pain by saying she wasn't as good in bed as his other girlfriend. "What other girlfriend?" was Nichole's obvious question. That was the first time she pieced together that Jim was seeing not just her but also another girl in the young adults group.

Jim had fallen into the trap of finding self-worth in the power of his position in ministry, a trap more common than most care to talk about. God had clearly gifted Jim with a heart for people, a hunger for study, and an amazing ability to convey God's truths to His people. But because Jim was raised without an ounce of God's grace in his spiritual foundation, he lived under the law. His legalism wouldn't allow him to be honest with God about his weaknesses.

All Jim knew to do was to try to be perfect for the kingdom's sake. God's Word tells us that the letter of the law kills, but the Spirit gives life (2 Cor. 3:6). For Jim the life of Christ that brings liberty was canceled out by the perfectionist performance the law demanded. Due to his inability to be honest with God about his needs, Jim was sliding down a slippery slope, taking vulnerable young girls down with him.

To add to the situation, Jim's marriage was unraveling. Carla had been raised by an alcoholic father. Her father's anger caused her to build up immense walls of fear and mistrust. Her fear drove her to ask and expect more of Jim than he could ever deliver. The more disappointed and disillusioned Carla became, the more it triggered Jim's worst fear: rejection.

In attempting to be perfect, Jim fell far from it. His misguided needs drove him to find approval from young women and to try to fill the void in his soul with their adoration. The very approval he craved ultimately led him to the deepest pit of rejection he could have ever imagined.

In spite of Jim's threats Nichole could no longer live with her guilt and came forward with the truth. She told the director of the women's ministry the entire sordid story. The director and the church elders confronted Jim, and he chose to lie, blaming Nichole's instability and reminding them of her numerous suicide attempts.

The elders pressed Jim further, asking him about the other girl Nichole told them about. He vehemently denied being intimate with anyone but Carla.

Wanting to give him the benefit of the doubt, the elders assured Jim that they would dig deeper into the allegations to bring resolve. They asked an impartial professional counselor to speak with each girl individually. Each of the girls' stories stacked up against Pastor Jim. The counselor came back to the elders with the disturbing news of striking similarities between the girls' experiences. In her professional opinion the girls were telling the truth.

The next confrontation with Jim and the elders began with more denial. It was only after the counselor stepped in with irrefutable details provided by the girls that Jim finally broke down, admitting he was guilty and the girls were indeed telling the truth.

Jim stepped down from his position as senior pastor, and he and Carla divorced.

Grieving the loss of Pastor Jim, Nichole woke up in room 118 at St. Mary's Hospital with her parents and two doctors at her bedside. This was her fourth attempted suicide, and they weren't going to let her out of their sight. She broke down in despair and told them about Pastor Jim. Her parents called the church immediately and spoke with the interim pastor. Heartbroken at the devastation in Nichole's life, the pastor called Mercy Ministries' Nashville office and spoke to me about taking in Nichole.

The first bed to open up for Nichole was in the Nashville home. I was pleased because I wanted to be personally involved in the process of her healing and transformation.

When she walked through the doors of Mercy, I wasn't prepared for what I saw. Nichole was so thin and frail that I wondered if we would need to put her back in the hospital before receiving her. Her eating, or lack thereof I should say, was her only source of control, and that need for control had nearly killed her. I sat with Nichole and tried to engage her in a conversation, but she was so depressed she couldn't speak.

Nichole's first challenge was to forgive all the people in her life, both past and present, who had wounded her.

Our challenge was helping her understand that although a spiritual leader who told her God had brought them together had manipulated her, she was an adult who chose to participate in sin. God sets before us life and death, and tells us to choose life (Deut. 30:19). It was important for Nichole to take responsibility for her part in the devastation and how she could have made better choices.

Abolishing the victim mentality in Nichole would be the key to returning her voice and power to her. Only then could she trust in God, who had never intended her to be with Jim. That relationship, like all the others Nichole had chosen, was beggars' bread compared to the banquet God was busy preparing for her to receive in the future. But first, Nichole needed healing and to be made whole. Only then would she feel deserving of such a banquet table. Only then could she be attracted to the kind of man God had in mind for her.

It breaks God's heart to see women like Nichole settle for so little.

Her next step was found in 1 John 1:9: "If we confess our sin, He is faithful and just to not only forgive us, but to cleanse us from all unrighteousness" (author's paraphrase). Because Mercy girls are so riddled with shame when they arrive, we make sure they learn the difference between shame and guilt. Guilt tells someone like Nichole, "I did something wrong." Shame tells her, "I *am* something wrong."

God intends conviction to usher in freedom and relief, not

shame. This truth is made clear in Psalm 103:10–12: "He has not dealt with us according to our sins, nor punished us according to our iniquities. For as the heavens are high above the earth, so great is His mercy toward those who fear Him; as far as the east is from the west, so far has He removed our transgressions from us."

Nichole's shame, first burned into her because of her father's harsh disapproval, drove her to compromise herself again and again. Guilt followed compromise and broke her in two. At Mercy, Nichole learned how to allow conviction to take her to a place of repentance, annihilating shame and bringing freedom.

Scripture tells us that God "is able to do exceedingly, abundantly above all that we ask or think, according to the power that works in us" (Eph. 3:20). Though we continually see God work in the lives of thousands of young girls day after day, month after month, and year after year, it never gets old, and we always stand in awe at what God is able to do. Nichole chose to surrender control and receive complete and total freedom from her eating disorder. She was able to do this because she chose to forgive Pastor Jim, her dad, and all the other men in her life who had wounded and disappointed her. She also chose to forgive herself. The power of God made that forgiveness stick as only He can.

When Nichole walked through the doors of Mercy Ministries, her eyes were vacant. After six months in the program, her eyes sparkled, and she was beaming with life and ready to graduate. Nichole stood in front of her family, shoulders held high, and shared her testimony, unashamed of how she surrendered her entire life to Christ to live for Him.

Her parents wept as she told about the powerful family counseling sessions that had taken place while she was at Mercy. Throughout Nichole's time with us, her parents visited her and offered their support, which helped Nichole work through the family dynamics that had contributed to her issues. Her father also wrote letter after letter asking forgiveness and offering his love and assurance. Nichole talked about how excited she was. For the first time in her life she felt loved and respected by her family. And she in turn loved and respected them more than she could say—a true miracle.

Talking about her plans after Mercy, Nichole mentioned nursing school and perhaps becoming a psychiatric nurse so that she could one day help young women who felt hopeless about their lives, just as she had. As is our custom at each Mercy graduation, the families were allowed to speak words of affirmation to their loved one if they so chose. Mike, Nichole's father, didn't hesitate. He stood up, walked to the front of the classroom, and hugged his daughter with tears streaming down his face, telling her this was the proudest day of his life. Laura, Nichole's mother, stayed in her seat, but thanked God over and over for answering the prayers she had prayed so long ago.

Nichole followed through with her desire to finish nursing school as a psychiatric nurse. Her first job was at St. Mary's psychiatric facility in Southern California, where she had been a patient after numerous suicide attempts. She was able to speak truth and hope to her patients in ways few people could.

While she was at St. Mary's, God used Nichole in mighty ways, and He didn't stop there. Her local church asked her to share her testimony with youth groups and young adults, again and again. I followed their lead and asked Nichole to come back from time to time to share her story at each of the Mercy homes in America. She was a great encouragement to our residents. Nichole was living proof that if God could change her life, He could change their lives as well.

While serving in her church and being an active volunteer ambassador for Mercy Ministries, Nichole began seeing a godly young man. They fell in love, and, for the first time, Nichole felt no fear of loss and abandonment. With God's love as its foundation, she could truly enjoy this new relationship. They became engaged and were married within two years of falling in love. Nichole's dad had the proud privilege of walking his beautiful daughter down the aisle, and both parents welcomed their new son-in-law with blessings. Nichole and her husband, Jake, are, at the time of this writing, expecting their second child and are very happy together.

It never ceases to amaze me how when God transforms one life, it affects so many others, including family, extended family, and close friends. Nichole's transformation confirms Isaiah 61:7, in which God proclaims that for your former shame, you will have double honor.

It has been more than a decade since the situation with Pastor Jim and Nichole. I am sure you must be wondering what happened to Pastor Jim.

After Pastor Jim acknowledged the truth, he became

MISSION OF MERCY

accountable to a select group of godly men and began the restoration process. Through this painful and difficult season God worked in Jim's heart to reveal and heal the roots of his moral failures and sin. The Bible tells us that "he who covers his sins will not prosper, but whoever confesses and forsakes them will have mercy" (Prov. 28:13).

Jim's willingness to go into counseling and address the wounds in his soul from the past allowed him to discover the difference between the letter of the law that kills and the Spirit that gives life. Legalism wrought perfectionism and people pleasing in Jim. It left him with no understanding of God's grace and His undeserved favor.

Legalism taught Jim to keep the outside covers in place while his inner man was shaky, riddled with fear of rejection, and filled with self-doubt. In counseling Jim learned that his marriage was fragile from the beginning. The intersection of two such broken lives had all the makings of a collision. Although God is more than able and willing to transform us, ignorance and unwillingness present huge roadblocks. Carla's upbringing in a highly dysfunctional home with an alcoholic father had resulted in thick defensive walls of fear and distrust. She either did not know or may have been unwilling to ask God for help. God's heart must break when His people perish for lack of knowledge (Hosea 4:6). But either way Carla's patterns of constant withdrawal triggered her husband's fear of rejection.

The harder Jim tried to perform for Carla, the more he felt like a failure. It wasn't long until the inadequacy he felt inside became a self-fulfilling prophecy and his fear manifested into utter failure. Only when his walls of perfectionism came tumbling down did Jim finally have the freedom to seek and receive the help he needed.

God's truth began to dispel every lie the enemy had used to prevent the grace of God from permeating Jim's life. Jim began to understand that a relationship with God is not only about keeping rules but also about knowing that apart from Him we can do nothing (John 15:5).

It would be easy to argue that Jim deserved to be punished for what he did to the two young women. Remember the story in the Gospel of John where a woman was caught in the act of adultery. The religious leaders of her town drug her through the streets, threw her at Jesus's feet, and demanded she be stoned to death for her sin, just as the law demanded. They were insisting that Jesus keep the rules instead of restoring the life. Jesus shut them down with seven words that have echoed throughout history: *"You without sin cast the first stone"* (John 8:7, author paraphrase). The religious leaders turned around and left.

The rule of the day said the punishment for adultery was death. Again, the letter of the law kills, but the Spirit gives life. Jesus came to display His heart for broken people and to show that mercy always triumphs over judgment. Regardless of *what* the sin may be or *who* the sinner is, God's heart is *always* to restore.

Now, more than a decade later, Jim is the senior pastor of a thriving and growing church in his community, not far from where he experienced his failure years before. He is happily married with a family and is doing great things to reach hurting and broken people and help them find hope and restoration. He understands compassion and has a heart for those who have made messes of their lives. No one knows better than Pastor Jim that God's heart is always to restore—*always!*

As in so many cases at Mercy, God gave me personal takeaways through Jim and Nichole. Seeing Nichole in a strong, healthy marriage after so many broken relationships built my faith to a higher level. God's power to restore extended far beyond the devastation of her past. Through Nichole, God once again proved to me that Jesus can restore *all* that has been stolen and wants to do so for every young woman who walks through the doors of Mercy.

At first, I saw *only* Nichole as a victim of circumstances. As I sought God, I saw both Jim and Nichole that way, but only after I recognized my judgmental spirit toward Jim. Who am I to decide whom God should forgive and whom *I* will forgive, for goodness' sake? The Bible tells me that I *must* forgive and that God *will* forgive anyone who confesses before His throne of grace.

I hate to admit it, but I was doubtful that Jim could ever be useful again behind the pulpit. But I couldn't ignore the truth found in Romans 11:29, that God's gifts and callings are irrevocable. I prayed for myself *and* Jim and watched God do His handiwork in Jim's life. I was blessed by Jim's courage to remain faithful to the ministry in his local community even though he knew that some people would forever judge him. Jim's courage challenged mine, and I began to speak up and stand for fallen leaders in my community and beyond.

I, like Jim before his fall, had deep pockets of religiosity in my life. This situation was the perfect opportunity for God to knock religiosity out of me and stretch my ability to forgive and believe the best for people like Jim. In time I was able to rejoice in Nichole's restoration and applaud and support Jim's as well.

Do you feel an *edge* toward Pastor Jim? I understand; I did too.

Let's remember King David. He committed adultery and then put his lover's husband on the front lines of the battle to be killed—nothing short of murder. David then took this fallen soldier's wife for his own. Later, God turned around and called David a man after His own heart. How is that possible? Because the Bible says David was quick to repent and God was quick to forgive. Let us not forget, however, that King David suffered consequences.

We have all made mistakes. All of us wish we could go back in time and change something we've done. But what's done is done, and that's where God steps in with forgiveness the moment we ask. He declares us not guilty—and who are we to disagree with God? God is so good that we can come to Him with *all* our issues and regrets. Proverbs 28:13 says that if we cover our sin, we will not prosper. But if we confess and forsake our sins, then we will be granted mercy. And the apostle Paul balances this out when he tells us we that must not sin frivolously, just because God's grace abounds (Rom. 6:1–2).

I learned to extend more mercy than previously and saw

both Nichole and Jim as pure, clean, and whole, just as God sees them. If I want God to see me this way, then I must be willing to see others as God does.

Galatians 6:1–2 in the Living Bible puts it this way:

> Dear brothers, if a Christian is overcome by some sin, you who are godly should gently and humbly help him back onto the right path, remembering that next time it might be one of you who is in the wrong. Share each other's troubles and problems, and so obey our Lord's command.

Bottom line, if I choose judgment over mercy, I am just like the legalistic rule keepers who were ready to stone the adulterous woman. Jesus wasn't pleased with them. And, more than anything else, I want to please Jesus. It is my reasonable offering for all He's done for me.

CHAPTER FIVE

The Great Exchange

NANCY, IT'S SUE. What does your watch say right now?"

"It's four forty-five," I answered.

I had no idea what my dear friend Sue was calling me about that afternoon, but I could tell by the tone in her voice that it was serious. Her voice was filled with compassion and conviction. Sue makes her living coaching young women on how to play their very best on the basketball court. Now she was coaching me on how to make this the very last day of limping down the court of life alone and in pain.

Nobody knows me as well as Sue does, so I listened carefully as she spoke. "OK. You have twenty-four hours to call one of these numbers. I've done my homework, Nancy, and these are the five best therapists in your area, and they are all Christians. I care too much about you to watch you struggle on your own. There's help out there, and it's time for you to find it."

Sue's not the mushy type, so her tender words made it difficult for me to say no or get defensive.

But I did get defensive. I kept my mouth shut, but my mind started needling me with a million reasons why this was a bad idea. "What are people going to think?" I couldn't help but question. But then I thought, "I am the head of Mercy Ministries, for goodness' sake, staffed by professional counselors. I can't be in trouble! I can't go to a counselor. I'm not supposed to have problems, am I? No, I'm just fine."

But before these fears could take root, I remembered Jim and Nichole. Their social-human casualty case had just come across my desk and was spreading like a wild fire through their circles of influence in Southern California. I didn't yet have the vantage point of seeing the beautiful ending God would write into their stories. I only saw the shattered pieces scattered across their lives. I wondered if Jim had a Sue. Did he have a friend like mine who tried to throw him a lifeline? Did Jim even try to take a hold of it? Did he drop it or maybe ignore it?

Even though thoughts of consequences about seeing a counselor scared me like crazy, what frightened me more was the reality of what happened to Jim and Nichole. It's funny how God works. His timing is always perfect to jolt me off my backside. It was time to deal with what I'd put off far too long.

I did continue to put it off, however. I stalled twenty-three hours and forty-five minutes to be exact. Yes, I can be a stubborn one. After Sue and I got off the phone the day before, I came up with a long list of reasons why I didn't need help. But out of respect for Sue and since she researched my area before calling me, I believed her concern was well founded. So fifteen minutes before the deadline, I made the appointment and called Sue back.

"OK, Sue. I did it," I said. "I just made my first counseling appointment. I know it's time. *Way* past time." And I knew it was. It was a relief to finally say those words, and I was glad Sue was the one to hear them.

"Way to go, Nance. I'm proud of you," Sue said so softly I almost couldn't hear her.

Going to a therapist for the first time is a mind game of the greatest sort. You walk in knowing you can't fool the specialist, yet you want to. You're hoping after a minute or two, you'll hear, "You're perfect, Nancy, a pillar of emotional and mental health! Let's go to lunch, shall we?" But no. My counselor, Margaret, sat there with this sweet blank stare on her face as I stumbled and blundered through my answers to her first three questions. Her pen, scribbling comments and notations about my life on a yellow legal pad, nearly caught fire from frantic friction.

I tried to ignore the scratching sound, and I know she did what she could to make me comfortable. Margaret had a sixth sense about how to put me at ease. She talked about Mercy and her respect for what we do. She told me she'd heard me speak and commented on my abilities to convey God's love and truth to His people. All this translated into my feeling safe and not too far off the path. I was immediately thankful for Margaret.

After some time had passed, she broke in with her first serious question: "Nancy, can you tell me what brought you to the place of seeking help from me?"

I wanted to blame it on Sue, but I knew better. I didn't have to think too hard to find the answer.

After taking a deep breath, I said, "Margaret, nine months ago my dad died. His death wasn't unexpected, but what caught me off guard was what it stirred up inside me. His death triggered feelings from all the losses I've suffered throughout my life. It took me back to the loss of my little sister, Beverly, and what my dad must have felt and gone through afterward. Now that I'm about the age he was when she died, I understand better how horrendous the trauma must have been for him. I can't seem to get up and over the grief of it all...the sadness I have for him. It isn't just what he lost, but what he and I never had at all."

Margaret smiled. "Nancy, when all the ways you've learned to cope stop working, it can feel hopeless. All the ways you've constructed to comfort yourself are falling apart. But if you could see this through God's eyes, you'd feel hope, even now. It's time, Nancy. God wants to give you a new coping kit. You have tried hard to cope on your own, but now you are going to have help, and He wants to complete that work. We hand Him our worn-out, bent, and broken tools, and He gives us a whole new coping kit. I call it 'the great exchange.'

"As a child we grab for whatever we can hold onto. The problem is *that* coping kit is made for survival. And this survival kit can sometimes work very well to get us through. But our worst and best day is when it no longer works. God doesn't want us to keep living in survival mode. He wants us to live in power.

"Yes, you have experienced more loss and more profound loss than most people. So one tool God wants to give you is compassion for yourself. We tend to be so afraid of feeling sorry for ourselves that we fail to acknowledge real pain and apply the compassion that could be soothing ointment to our painful wounds. If you remember, in the story of the feeding of the five thousand, Jesus looked at the crowds and was filled with compassion. He also wept over Jerusalem. I believe this was also birthed out of His compassion. You once had a tree that sheltered you and offered you compassion when your little sister died, but the unseen figure sitting next to you that day was Jesus, who was there to comfort you.

"During the time of your family's losses, the tendency was not to talk and cry together, but to 'be strong,' which carried messages such as 'keep a stiff upper lip' and 'you've got to keep going.' At the time it seemed noble to think this way, and it was all you knew to do. You weren't given any other option, so you bottled up the pain again and again and got really good at it, in fact. Your pain became layered, Nancy, and each layer calloused over so that you could continue doing what you love…seeing broken lives transformed by the power of God. But now it's time to allow Him to do a deeper work in *you*."

Margaret then took out her Russian stacking dolls. She pulled them apart and demonstrated the analogy that all the parts reside unseen—each with its own stored feelings, thoughts, joys, and sorrows—but the only one I could see was the doll on the outside.

"We are going to learn to minister to all these parts, Nancy," Margaret said. "We will start with the young girl, then the young woman, and finally the woman you are today. We are going to listen to the hurt and acknowledge that it is real. You and God are going to do for those parts what was missing at the time of the losses."

We ended that first session in prayer, and Margaret sat quietly with me and allowed the Holy Spirit to settle over us. She assured me that He would walk with me through this entire process.

My first hour in professional counseling was over. I'd made it through. When I left that day, I had hope for a new tomorrow and a life free from the fear of loss.

As soon as I got home I called Sue and told her how well it had gone. She was thrilled and asked when I'd be going back to see Margaret again. I told her I had an appointment for the next week. It was in that moment I realized this journey of deep healing would take time. Sometimes we pray and God miraculously and instantly fixes the need we've brought before Him, but in most cases it takes time for the healing to happen.

The word *healing* denotes process. When I get a deep cut

on my hand, it doesn't heal overnight. The same is true of the wounds of the soul and spirit. If we expect otherwise, we set ourselves up for disappointment and can even lose heart in our faith in God.

When I hung up the phone with Sue, I knew that this journey would be long and filled with pain, joy, and finally...relief.

God wanted to lead me through the root causes and the core issues underlying my anger. And, yes, unexplained anger was next on God's agenda for me. I was barely over the angst from my first counseling appointment when God turned up the flame beneath the anger buried in my heart.

Like many of us, I believe I was guilty of trying to take a spiritual shortcut instead of digging into the pain of anger and allowing healing to come to me.

In hindsight I understand what is made so clear in Psalm 23:3–4 (AMP):

> He refreshes and restores my life (my self); He leads me in the paths of righteousness [uprightness and right standing with Him—not for my earning it, but] for His name's sake. Yes, though I walk through the [deep, sunless] valley of the shadow of death, I will fear or dread no evil, for You are with me; Your rod [to protect] and Your staff [to guide], they comfort me.

He is refreshing and restoring my life, and that includes my past (v. 3). He tells me I am to walk *through* the valley of the shadow of death, not around it (v. 4). Confessing the Word of God is vital in the transformation we all seek as followers of

Christ, but it must be balanced with pressing into the painful parts of our past that still need healing. The Great Physician draws us close to His skillful hands, and we are completely healed when He is finished. And we are more in love with Him than ever for the work He has accomplished in our time together.

How much more priceless is the healing when it has served to deepen our personal relationship with God! Certainly any one of us would rather avoid the valley of pain, but to short-circuit this process would be to rob ourselves of experiencing God's love and tender heart. Without the still waters of truly knowing God, we continue to go around and up and down the same mountain of pain, time and time again.

The next week I entered Margaret's office ready to walk through the valley of my unexplained anger. I expressed to her how frustrated I was with blowing up at people over the littlest things, quickly apologizing, all the while knowing that it would happen again and again. Margaret jumped in, backed by God and her years of wisdom.

"Nancy, when you were little and no one was there to help you process your grief, it was like an infection left to fester in the wound. An infection like that is nasty stuff, and if it stays in the wound too long, it turns to gangrene, which is poisonous to the system—poisonous to the soul and spirit.

"There are probably many themes inside you that have become trigger points for anger (infection) to be released. We call those places that hold infection 'pain pockets.' They sit right beneath the surface. You and I will work to keep identifying them. What we know now is that you have experienced tangible losses, deep disappointments, injustices—unfortunate things that should not have happened.

"One cause of anger is *unmet expectation*. I like to make distinctions between legitimate and illegitimate expectations, and most of your losses fall into the category of legitimate unmet expectations.

"It was OK to expect your little sister to grow up alongside you and your other siblings, and it was OK to expect your boyfriend to go on to college and take advantage of his scholarship. Nancy, do you remember Dr. Kübler-Ross, the expert on death and dying who teaches on the stages of grief? She helped us break down grief into bite-size pieces that include shock (I can't believe this just happened), anger (It did happen and I am angry about it), sadness (I am so sad that it happened), and finally, acceptance. Sometimes we get stuck in the anger stage.

"When living in the anger stage, daily disappointments much smaller than the loss of Beverly can trigger the opening of the pain pocket. To compound the issue, Nancy, you seem to focus on what people *should* do or how things *ought* to happen around you. Sometimes these are valid expectations about what people should do; sometimes they're not. Your challenge now is to rewire your way of thinking to make sure your expectations are not rooted in illegitimate pain pockets. During this time you're going to need to hold life loosely in your hands.

"The serenity prayer will become one of your well-worn prayers and a good friend in these times: *God, grant me the serenity to accept the things I cannot change, the courage to change the things I can, and the wisdom to know the difference.* Picture your open hands, not grasping for a specific outcome. And along with this practice we will keep cleaning out the wounds, and you will learn the triggers and what lies beneath them. It is a process. That is why I call it grief work."

My sessions with Margaret were like being in a spiritual and emotional ICU. They were difficult but brought such relief. I got better and better at opening up to both Margaret and God about anything the Holy Spirit brought to mind in between our sessions. It didn't take long before I knew way ahead of time just where God wanted to go next.

My next issue was what I like to call the "workhorse treadmill." Bottom line, I felt used and overworked. I knew I was the biggest contributor to the problem but didn't know how to fix it. I also knew that God did not call me to ministry to run myself ragged, so I asked Margaret why I was doing this to myself. "Nancy, I am so glad you are identifying these things and that you can put them into words. God is working hard to reveal and heal you as the months go by. Remember that you grew up in a large family with many children. I am sure there were times you would like to have had a voice and some voting power, but there were so many children and voices to be heard.

"I am sure you did lots of right things, performed lots of duties just because you had to. Sometimes there were other opinions and thoughts and feelings inside of you that had to be squashed. I expect that those now cause some inner conflict, which I call ambivalences—vying parts inside. Things can get very confusing. "I do what I *should* do" runs through your head wrestling against thoughts like, 'What about me? What do I want? Am I just here to serve you?'

"Then comes the counterpart thought saying, 'Oh, but I am not supposed to want anything for me, and I am supposed to die to myself.' So you do what you think is right and feel guilty for wanting more. You leave yourself no option but to stuff your sense of obligation and exhaustion back down inside you. I am sure a lot of this went on in your head while growing up in that very large family of yours, 'I want, but everyone looks so over-burdened that I surely can't put more on these people' and 'I must be bad for wanting more.'"

Margaret went on, "Again, the old, early paradigms get in the way. God does want our obedience. He does want us to be His hands and feet on the earth, but at the same time He wants to hear from His children. In Matthew 11:28 Jesus said, 'Come to Me, all who are weary and heavy-laden, and I will give you rest' [NAS]. In Zephaniah 3:17 the Word says, 'God will rejoice over you with gladness, He will quiet you with His love, and He will rejoice over you with singing' [author's paraphrase]. What He is saying there is that He is all about His children! It is the same in parenting. We may need our children to do their chores and be obedient, but hopefully when they tug on our shirts wanting to tell us something, we bend down and listen to their wants and needs.

"Nancy, this is very sad, but I don't think you ever tugged on your parents' shirts or pant legs. I think they looked so burdened, you didn't learn to express longings, wants, and needs. But today God is bending over to listen to you. Your wants and needs are there, because you are human. So now, after so long, God wants you to tell Him about all the things you want, things you hope for. If you can talk, He *will* listen."

One of the last issues I brought to Margaret's attention was a terrifying pattern that would haunt me from time to time. I began by describing one particular scenario that occurred in the early years of Mercy Ministries when I was living in Louisiana. A dear friend from Virginia came to spend a long holiday weekend with me. At the end of her visit I dropped her off at the airport.

"Time to get back to the work of the ministry," I thought as I got in my car to drive away. But that is when the unwelcome intruder broke into my thoughts like a thief on the take—and "taking" was an understatement. Without warning I was hit with a scene not unfamiliar to me. It was like going to watch a familiar play, only with different actors.

Like other times before and since, I was convinced my friend would die that day in a plane crash. It was so real to me that I actually drove home and turned on the TV, waiting for the news bulletin of the plane crash to flash across the screen. After two hours of staring at a program I was not even really watching, I began to realize that once again I had been "taken."

After I finished, Margaret said, "Nancy, this might not seem normal to you, to have these fears and thoughts, but in the context of what you have experienced, they are extremely normal and very understandable. There are threads woven into your mind through very real experiences that we would call 'catastrophic thinking.' This kind of thinking makes you reexperience trauma just as if you were there, and it is very common in the aftermath of trauma. It is one of the symptoms of post-traumatic stress.

"You are experiencing flashbacks and flashforwards. These are all in the natural realm, but there is another realm to be aware of, and that is the spiritual realm. This battle is on another level. I believe that Satan wants to use these 'openings' to torment you. If given the opportunity, he can flash pictures on the screen of your mind in order to torment you. It is as though he says, 'Well, look at that, and that, and that.' So during these times we will also have to fight spiritual battles as well as the natural one.

"It is helpful to think of your mind as a computer. If you never clean your hard drive and replace what's there with God's Word, the damaging thoughts and lies from the past will appear on the screen in times of need. At Mercy, you call it 'replacing lies with truth.' With post-traumatic stress, it is common to have intrusive thoughts, ones that just come, more from the outside than the inside.

"When this happens, you need to imagine your computer mouse as a trap and your hard drive as a cage. Grab the thoughts and take them captive before they are allowed to infect your heart, your mind, and influence your actions. This is your responsibility, Nancy, to do as 2 Corinthians 10:5–6 tells us to, 'and we take captive every thought to make it obedient to Christ, and cast down vain imaginations' [paraphrase].

"You see, the Bible says we are not to have 'vain imaginations' and 1 Corinthians 2:16 tells us that we have the mind of Christ. God created the imagination, and we can use His Word to harness our thoughts and fill our minds with hope for a future of promise, not the fear that comes from the what-ifs we dream up. This takes practice. Practice makes perfect in abolishing old mental habits that cause us harm. And it's all part of the restoration process."

Understanding why I was dreaming up disasters helped me to stop doing it, almost immediately. It's amazing what a little knowledge can do. I can remember having trouble at the free-throw line when I was playing basketball. I'd dribble the ball three times, and right before I'd shoot the ball, I'd lock my knees. I'd miss the shot every time until my coach told me to breathe and keep my knees supportive but slightly bent before shooting the ball.

One little observation from my coach made all the difference in the world. I made most of my free throws from that point on. Going to a good, solid, Christian counselor like Margaret is no different. We all need another set of eyes from time to time to assist with things we are too close to see for ourselves.

My last session with Margaret that year was right before the holidays. Soon Thanksgiving and Christmas would arrive, and I was thankful that God had done so much for me through my times with Margaret. The holidays can bring out the worst in us. It seems emotions that we keep at bay all year fight their way to the surface during the holiday season. I prayed, asking God to bring to mind what He wanted to help me with, and it was clear that my tendency to draw close to people and then turn around and push them away was what He wanted to work on.

I sat in the waiting area in Margaret's office and felt nothing but peace that had come from the hard work we'd already done that year. When I sat down in what I call "the healing chair" and told Margaret what was on my mind, she dove right in.

"The desire, Nancy, for attachment is one of the strongest we have. You have seen and experienced the tiny fingers of a baby grasping one of yours. It is automatic. The baby is born to 'move toward.' It is only through hurt that we begin to move away. Hurt and pain say 'move away' not 'move toward,' but each day of healing brings back the desire to move toward and grasp, trust, and believe for the best in people. Hurt and fear make us overcautious and become a breeding ground for 'come-here and go-away' messages.

"We know that God moved toward man and woman. He, in fact, was somewhat of a maddened lover if you read Song of Solomon. His love moved toward Israel again and again. They would betray Him, and He would offer them chance after chance for restoration and reconciliation. Remember how we talked about the normalcy of wanting and longing? So we reach back for our tool of compassion, trying to identify what part of us wants to move toward and what part wants to move away. Obviously the wounded and fearful parts, the parts that don't want to lose again, are pulling on you to move away saying, 'Don't get too close. They might go away.'

"This is where we get to pull a useful tool from that strong, truth-based survivor kit inside. We use the tool of courage. Moses told Joshua as he was preparing him to take new land to 'be strong and of good courage.' A relationship must be formed between your courageous parts and fearful parts so that on this bridge, you can walk across to the other side. These will be reconciled and eventually of one mind even though a remnant of fear may be there at times. When this happens, you can smile and feel thankful for the days gone by when the voice of fear was so loud inside you that you couldn't ignore it.

"The voices of understanding, patience, and tolerance are soothing to the soul. Learning to love yourself is an exercise of faith and believing God's promises. In Mark 12:31 Jesus said, 'Love your neighbor as yourself.' So loving yourself is key to loving the people around us."

I sat and allowed Margaret's words to soak into my soul and my spirit. Loving myself wasn't something I'd ever taken time to think about. As a child I was too busy staying out of the way. And later in life ministry became my deepest passion. The sad truth is that I'd gotten great at helping others see their value, but I didn't know my own worth.

The first year of counseling began seven years of this process. *Seven!* God's perfect number of completion. It's fitting really, but not because I feel complete. If counseling has taught me anything at all, it's taught me that I'll never be completely whole until I enter heaven's gates. I don't know what I don't know, but God's Word tells me that wisdom is more priceless than silver or gold. And those who seek *will* find. (See Proverbs 16:16; Jeremiah 29:13.) And so I will keep seeking wisdom and embrace the fact that there is more for me to learn and most importantly that it's OK to admit the need to improve, the need to be healed, and the need to need.

Where and when did we Christians adopt the belief that we

should never have a flaw, a fault, or a need? I can't find that requirement in Scripture anywhere. In fact, I find just the opposite to be true. The apostle Paul wrote: "[His] strength is made perfect in [my] weakness" (2 Cor. 12:9). And "when I am weak, then I am strong" (v. 10) seems to be more like what God is asking of us.

Going to Margaret was like cracking open the thin shell of an egg and allowing the yolk to fall out, drop on the floor, and spread. It was a relief to stop juggling the fragile little egg, trying to prevent it from breaking through the perils of my life.

So it broke. So what? It wasn't nearly as big a deal as I thought it would be. And with the breaking came freedom from the yoke of bondage I'd worn for so long trying to hold everything inside.

Why is it that we as leaders are so afraid to let people know that we are "just people"? It is clear that God's anointing rains down on leaders as they take the platform to speak the truth of His Word, but when we step down from the platform, we are not entitled to some sort of special anointing to help us walk out the Word of God in our lives just because we are leaders or ministers. We must walk it out every day like every other believer in Christ.

It was 2002 when Sue first challenged me to get help for my pain, and I shudder to think what might have happened had I not taken her advice. One of the reasons I decided to go to counseling was I knew professional counselors are bound by laws of confidentiality. I felt safe knowing our words would go no further than the four walls of Margaret's office.

It wasn't long, however, before God began challenging me to share about my counseling sessions with my staff and even the Mercy residents. I said things such as: "Even though I am leading a ministry, I am still in the process of transformation just like everyone else." As I opened up so did they, and freedom became contagious throughout the Mercy homes. Many of the staff and girls in the program knocked on my office door and poured out their hearts about things they would have never shared previously.

I became so free in opening up to others about what I was receiving in counseling that I began sharing it while speaking in large conferences in America and around the world. At every opportunity I told people about the hope that comes from God through gifted people like Margaret, and I prayed they also would give themselves permission to find help if they felt the need to do so.

One thing I know for sure: if we do not deal with our issues, at some point our issues will deal with us. I also know God will always deal with a person privately before He exposes them publicly. It is not God's will for any of His children to be publicly humiliated. But too often leaders have to step down from ministry simply because they did not seek the help and accountability they needed before things went too far.

I challenge you to let go of shame and fear and to have the courage to walk boldly down the path of restoration. Remember the story of blind Bartimaeus in Mark 10:46–52? He cried out through the crowd, begging Jesus for help. The crowd told Bartimaeus to hush up. It would have been easy for Bartimaeus to become fearful of what others were saying and stop calling out. But he ignored their opinions and cried out until Jesus said, "Call him here."

No sooner had the Lord acknowledged Bartimaeus than the crowd swapped leads and cheered the blind man forward to take courage and find healing from the Messiah. Jesus healed Bartimaeus telling him, "Your faith has made you well" (v. 52). I'd say so. Bartimaeus's biggest step of faith was keeping his eyes focused on Jesus and ignoring the discouraging cries from the crowd.

I am being transparent and making myself vulnerable in writing this book. It breaks my heart when I see my friends forced to step down from what God has called them to do because they felt the same way I felt before my friend Sue challenged me to get help. I'm sure they thought, "What will people think?" and "I'm supposed to be the leader." Ministry leaders are no different from other people in needing godly counsel. There is no room for the fear of losing our place in ministry because we choose to seek help.

When I began to open up about going to counseling, people began taking off their masks and sharing things that blew me away. When we get real with people, people get real with us. If we wear masks and façades with other people, then we get masks and façades back. God wants us to have genuine and authentic relationships, not just with Him but also with each other.

I pray that other ministry leaders will seek help in godly counseling and not succumb to the fear of losing their jobs and reputations. I have found that being a leader who goes to counseling has not diminished people's respect for me but has caused me to gain respect. This is my prayer for you as well. Like Bartimaeus, stand up in the crowd, speak out, take courage, and watch Jesus heal the blindness hidden deep within your soul.

CHAPTER SIX

White Stones

I F YOU HAVE ever wondered how far the hand of God can
reach, how deep and wide His healing balm can seep into
the human soul, meet Camillia. She walked through the
doors of the St. Louis Mercy home on August 24, 2010, and
graduated the program in March 2011.

When I think of Camillia's journey, I can't help but think
of the apostle John, the author of the last book in the Bible,
Revelation, written when John was ninety-two. Camillia was

twenty-nine when she wrote the letter you are about to read. John and Camillia were different in age but not in need. God designed them both to be oracles of hope for the faithful and to sound the alarm to the lost and faithless.

Like Camillia, the apostle John was imprisoned by man and yet free in every other sense. The authorities thought they were in control of these two saints, but God was in charge, and He alone determined what would become of them.

John was sent to the remote barren penal colony of Patmos, a rocky island in the Aegean Sea. The authorities made the mistake of thinking they could silence God's voice in John by sending him to this forsaken island. But his banishment provided him the quiet needed to hear from God.

Camillia's wounds drove her to Mercy Ministries, and there she pressed her ear to God's chest and intensely listened to His voice, just as John did on Patmos.

John and Camillia were both tortured. Tradition says before Patmos, the apostle was dipped in boiling oil and when miraculously he didn't die, they sent him away to silence him. Before Mercy, Camillia's enemy tried to silence her, methodically disassembling her soul with a tyranny beyond imagination, right under her own roof. Her escape wasn't as quick as John's, but it was just as miraculous as surviving a vat of boiling oil. In the end, neither John nor Camillia was silenced. They are two of God's finest, separated by more than two thousand years.

Here is Camillia's story straight from her heart.

I was born January 10, 1982, in Georgetown, Washington DC. During my early childhood years I lived on the outskirts of a town called Herndon, Virginia. My father was an Episcopal youth pastor and public speaker, and my mother was a stay-at-home mom. I have two half-brothers and one half-sister from my father's first marriage, but we've never really had a relationship, and growing up they were never mentioned. From the outside everything looked great. We lived in a nice neighborhood, my parents were respected in the community, and I went to a great school. But behind closed doors it was a different picture. My father abused my mother emotionally, mentally, verbally, and sometimes physically. Watching him treat my mother the way he did made me terrified of him.

There was *always* an undertone of fear and strife in our home because you never knew what little thing might set him off. One night my mother and I returned home from a wedding we had attended without my father, and I made the mistake of telling him Mom danced with someone at the reception. He tore off her dress and threw her out into the snow. Other times he flipped things over while ranting, raving, and cussing at my mother for random pointless reasons. I wanted his love, attention, and approval but could not get past the fear. It didn't make much difference because my father didn't have time for me anyway.

We were part of a well-known Episcopal church in the area, where my father pastored teenagers who were very enamored of

77

him. It was a unique upbringing because we were the only black family there. As long as people were around, my mom and I were safe because my father wanted to make a good impression.

When I was five or six years old, I started getting migraine headaches every Sunday morning when I knew I was going to have to watch him preach love and grace in church while at home we were living in hell. Nothing made sense to me, especially God, because I knew He must be just like my dad.

My dad was the most charismatic man I had *ever* met. When he walked into a room, people took notice. He was an impeccable dresser, extremely articulate, and *very* handsome. Trying to guess what his malfunction was, the only conclusion I came to was that he never healed from his own abusive past. Prior to meeting my mother he had just been released from prison.

While my father was in prison, Billy Graham came and spoke, and my father received Christ. Also while in prison, my father met a man named Chuck Colson, who had been released from prison a few years earlier and had just founded an organization called Prison Fellowship. He was impressed with my father and offered him a job as soon as he was released. While working for Mr. Colson, my father met my mother, and they got married three months later.

Over the next few years my father appeared on *Face the Nation* with Billy Graham, spoke all over the country, ministered to sports teams, and made a name for himself. The sad thing is he allowed making a name for himself to take precedence over admitting that he was in pain and needed help. I quickly learned by observation that what goes on behind closed doors stays behind closed doors, and in public you put a smile on your face and play the part.

The seeds of needing acceptance at all cost and the fear of rejection were planted in me. I learned to ignore my true emotions and became confused by all the different masks I was developing. Anger was an emotion I mistakenly thought was "bad" and that I should ignore. I covered up everything by being outgoing.

One extremely terrifying thing my father did was to threaten suicide. Every time he threatened suicide, my mother would beg him not to do it. When I think of how she was in their marriage, I now know it's called codependency. It was a sick, vicious cycle of abuse, suicide threats, him apologizing to never do it again, peace for a few months, and then it would begin all over again.

By the time I was eight years old, my father had an opportunity to pastor and counsel at a church in Mount Vernon, New York, as well as be the chaplain for their police department. I found it ironic that my dad was offering help to so many while he was the one who was truly sick.

The summer of 1990 we made the move, and almost immediately things went from bad to worse. At Christmas time my father had another one of his rages, and my mother finally put her foot down and called the police . . . the same police my father was working for. For a while after that we stayed with my grandmother. My father called all the time. One time he almost overdosed, and I ended up on the phone with him. I remember screaming for him to stay awake while my mom ran to call the police on another line, terrified that he was going to die.

At this point my family's secrets were beginning to leak out, and my father decided to seek help at a pastors' treatment center in Colorado. Approximately three months later my mother decided to give my father another chance. We returned to New York, and my father began working at another church in New York City.

I was nine years old, and during the next couple of years I began displaying my own violent tendencies toward other kids. My father's rages returned, this time at a more intense level. He became more violent toward my mom. One night she got mad at my father because of a broken promise he had made to me. In retaliation, he choked her with a telephone cord while I stood in the doorway and watched. Another night around that same time I awoke to my mother crying, asking my father to leave her alone as he raped her.

A short time later—I'll never forget it, it was Egyptian Day at school and we were all dressed in our fun outfits—my mother pulled up in our car packed top to bottom with our things. I knew what that meant. I never would see my classmates again. My mother ended up having to get a police escort back to our house to pick up a few things. The last memory I have of my father is sitting on his lap crying and saying good-bye.

Two weeks later my father made good on his threats and hung himself. When I found out, I remember not knowing how to express the emotions I was feeling, so I just acted like I had been programmed to and pretended everything was OK.

When I saw the report on TV about my father's suicide, I felt numb. At my father's funeral back in Virginia, Chuck Colson gave the eulogy and people gave their condolences, but after that I don't remember anyone ever contacting us again. Just like that, everyone was gone. I was hurt, angry, and confused, and all I knew to do was stuff it down inside.

That summer we moved to Virginia Beach to be near my mother's family. By fall I was back in school like nothing ever happened. To be honest, at that point I "forgot" about my father. It was too painful to remember. By now Satan had worked to convince me that I was worthless, unloved, abandoned, and basically defective.

Over the next ten years my life became progressively more and more chaotic. By age thirteen I had lost my virginity. By age fifteen I was smoking marijuana and drinking. By the end of my senior year I had slept with more guys than I would like to remember. I was hospitalized in a mental institution three times for attempted suicide and diagnosed bipolar, borderline personality disorder, ADD, ADHD, and some other things I can't remember. I was locked up in juvenile hall for stealing my mother's car.

Throughout this time my mother continued taking me to different churches doing her best to expose me to Christ. I've been an Episcopalian, Baptist, evangelical, and some other ones in between. We even went to a small church gathering where they decided I was possessed and tried to rebuke the devils out of me. To put it mildly, the last thing I wanted to be associated with was Christians or Jesus.

At age nineteen I decided to move in with a friend in Richmond, Virginia, where I attended a community college. My first priority was to dive into the local party scene, which I accomplished quite successfully. I also became involved with a drug dealer who initially was just a friend. Over the next year or so we became sexually involved. One night I told him I did not want to have sex, but as far as he was concerned that was not an option, and he raped me. I wish I could say that I stopped seeing him, but I didn't. I had no self-esteem, and he exposed me to a lifestyle that I believed I wouldn't have without him.

Over the next few years I continued to be promiscuous. I met a guy while working at a bar, started seeing him, and quickly became pregnant. I didn't see any other option than to have an abortion, so I did. Within the next few months I became pregnant again by the same guy and had a second abortion. We ended up living together, and over the next two years the relationship became abusive, both emotionally and verbally. Eventually it became physically abusive.

By age twenty-three I had been fired from my bartending job and felt utterly hopeless. One day while sitting in my apartment alone I ended up watching Christian television. At the end of the program they asked viewers about receiving salvation. For whatever reason, I said, "Why not?" I began attending church immediately and making better decisions, but I was still an emotional wreck. I had a *very* legalistic view of God. One night out of desperation, I got down on my knees and prayed for some place to get help for free because I had no money. Two weeks later I received a Joyce Meyer magazine in the mail, and there was an article about Mercy Ministries inside. I was high when I went online and requested an application.

I was on the waiting list for a season of time, but when a spot finally opened, I was so relieved. I wanted to be "fixed," so no matter what it took, I was willing to try. The crazy thing is I didn't even realize I was angry until after I had been at Mercy a few weeks. I knew I was dysfunctional, but I never labeled it as anger. Over the first few months I was all about working hard, but with time the more I tried to "work," the more I realized that I was trying to fix myself and not allowing God the opportunity. As I realized this, I slowly began to give up control and ended up understanding that I had *no* idea of the concept of grace. How could God actually love me after everything I had done? I had been told how much God loved me but had never received it as a personal heart revelation.

What I've learned is that it comes down to Him loving me because He wants to. Period. Just because I've believed otherwise all my life doesn't make it true. Every time I hurt, Jesus hurts too. His grace has been one of the biggest blessings I've ever received. I have also learned about His mercy. That was demonstrated through the staff at Mercy; they knew my past and accepted me as I was.

The other thing God has continued to demolish in me is fear. I learned to stop focusing on me so much and focus on Him and His

Word. No matter what, He and His Word don't change. The biggest fear I had was of rejection because of my father, but what I've come to learn—though not easily—is that it's none of my business if people reject me. My job is to love God and love others and to be obedient to what He tells me to do.

Just because someone hurts or rejects me doesn't mean that I have to respond. I can go to God because He is my defender, my refuge, and my strong tower. Though it is an ongoing process through learning the truth about God and His Word, I have been able to forgive the people who have hurt me as well as forgive myself. As I continue to delve deeper into my revelation of His love, I am able to get a clearer picture of who He truly is, and as this happens He is continuing to set me free. One thing I know for sure: if I had not reached out to Mercy Ministries for help, I would be dead.

As we read Camillia's heartbreaking story, we can't help but wonder how on earth God fixed in seven months what took twenty-nine years to become so twisted, so broken, so bruised. I must admit, even after thirty years of watching God transform Mercy girl after Mercy girl, it comes down to putting my faith in the power of God's living Word and not in human statistics. His promises are not empty. These girls prove this every time I believe for them to be made new.

When Camillia came to Mercy, the first thing I noticed was her timidity. Considering her serious issues, you wouldn't think that her quietness would concern me so much, but it did. In the Book of Revelation John wrote: "And they overcame him by the blood of the Lamb and by the *word* of their testimony" (Rev. 12:11, emphasis added).

If we can't speak words of power, we are doomed to be powerless by words of defeat, bitterness, and unforgiveness—damaging words like the ones Camillia endured from her father. His words shut her down, shut her up, and made her believe she was helpless and worthless. How he treated her mother sent her the message that men are allowed to use women and discard them when they are finished with them. From a young age Camillia was like a wounded animal, prey to every enemy that smelled her fear.

God spoke this world into existence. And Scripture tells us that if you confess with your mouth "Jesus is Lord" and believe in your heart that God raised him from the dead, you will be saved (Rom. 10:9). Speaking is as important as believing.

Words matter. Speaking them matters even more.

Of all Camillia's losses, losing her words to her bully of a father was the most debilitating. Her counselors at Mercy recognized this immediately and began speaking boldness over her from day one. At first she had no idea why they were so intent on praying this way. But their prayers dislodged her tongue, and her confessions of faith soon became like ramrods against the remnants of her childhood abuse.

And from there God did what most people would believe impossible—He revealed to Camillia His beautiful fatherhood and claimed her as His beloved daughter. She learned that He was trustworthy, and this built a strong foundation of strength for her concept of herself as a woman and as a human being. When we know God the Father as well as we know the Son and Holy Spirit, we have the entire Godhead and all His benefits working in our lives. Without an intimate relationship with the Father, we can only limp along in our faith.

At Mercy, Camillia began to feel whole and complete, which produced rapid and permanent changes in her. Her relationship with the Father wasn't something that would be here briefly and then disappear. It was eternal and eclipsed her broken past. Sadly some people never come to know the Father in the way Camillia did, and they let months drain into years of additional loss and defeat. But for Camillia, her newfound security produced fruit for all of us to see, and she was finally free from the past. God the Father was finally the only one she needed or wanted.

While Camillia was hard at work at Mercy, her ex-boyfriend, Paul, was working on his life as well. Camillia and Paul broke up before she came to Mercy. She had known it was time to cut all ties with the past and trust God with her future. Letting go of Paul was the hardest part for Camillia. Paul prayed for Camillia and read many of the same books she was reading. He even checked in with her counselors from time to time to see how she was doing. It was apparent to all of us that Paul carried no specific agenda in his concern for Camillia. He knew he was as unhealthy as she was and was trusting God with his future. He wrote Camillia a letter expressing all that God was doing in his life but asked that it not be given to her until she was "in a good place." He trusted the counselors to do as they thought best for her.

Right before Camillia was about to return home for Christmas break, her counselor handed Camillia Paul's letter and said, "I think it's time for you to read this. Paul sent it to me to give to you as God would lead."

Camillia's eyes filled with tears as she read Paul's words of love and encouragement without a single request for himself. Many things had happened in Paul's life by the hand of God, including finding a great job in Washington DC. So while she had been praying for him, he had been praying for her, and neither one knew the other was praying. Scripture challenges men to love their wives as Christ loved the church and gave Himself for it (Eph. 5:25). Paul displayed this kind of love for Camillia, not knowing if she would ever be his wife, not knowing if he would ever see her again.

What a great way to restart a relationship. After the trauma Camillia had experienced, it was wonderful to watch God give Camillia, in Paul, the exact opposite of her father.

God is a God of details. He knows the desires of our hearts and how we are wired. He knows exactly what we need to replace what the locusts have eaten (Joel 2:25).

Paul and Camillia were married on July 31, 2011, with Paul's grandfather and father presiding over their union. How perfect to see fatherhood as it was designed by God sprinkled all around as they became one in the Lord. I have to believe that the Father Himself stood by proudly, admiring His work in Paul and Camillia.

The apostle John wrote God's words in the quiet of Patmos, words that would one day unlock Camillia's silence. In the middle of John's own persecution, he penned words to *the persecuted* of future generations, not the least of whom was Camillia.

With her voice now unleashed, she speaks boldly wherever and whenever God calls her. Camillia has truly overcome by the blood of the Lamb and the word of her testimony. We at Mercy are privileged to have her video testimony on our website found at Mercyministries.com. She speaks to crowds of more than twenty thousand people. Paul and Camillia are monthly donors to Mercy Ministries, giving back financially and in so many other ways.

That's the kind of God we serve. He's able to use a ninety-two-year-old man and a twenty-nine-year-old woman to show Himself faithful to the faithful and to give warning to the ones He loves just as much, the ones He cries out for—like Camillia's father.

John's words sum it up best:

> He who has an ear, let him hear what the Spirit says to the churches. To him who overcomes I will give some of the hidden manna to eat. And I will give him a white stone, and on the stone a new name written which no one knows except him who receives it.
>
> —REVELATION 2:17

May we, like Camillia and Paul, be found with a white stone in our pockets, with a new life in our hearts, and with a new Father. And may He be our One, our only—our everything.

CHAPTER SEVEN

The Third Option

THIS LYRIC, AN obscure verse in the well-known and beloved song "Jesus Loves Me," is not one many of us sang as little ones. More than likely, you've never heard it before, but it's the perfect fit for Michele.

> Jesus loves me—loves me still,
> Though I'm very weak and ill;
> From his shining throne on high
> Comes to watch me where I lie.

Yes, Jesus loves me
Yes, Jesus loves me
Yes, Jesus loves me
The Bible tells me so.

—Anna Bartlett Warner
and Sarah Warren[1]

I am proud of every Mercy girl, but Michele is one whose story astounds me. The world would call her "a one in a million who beat the odds," but I see Michele as someone who knew how to seek God before she even knew His name. Michele is a young woman who knew when to cry out to God, and when she did, God was right there to meet her exactly where He found her, exactly as the sweet lyric describes it.

Sit back and read Michele's touching story, and prepare to be blessed.

I was four years old. I heard the screen door slam. I froze. I held tight to my Cabbage Patch doll, cradling her in my arms like a newborn baby and breathing in her faint baby powder smell. I was frantic. I knew I had very little time. I listened and watched for clues that would help me know what to do. Was I safe or in danger? Was it OK to stay where I was playing, or should I run and hide? I surveyed my options for nearby hiding places. There were several around the house that I had spent hours practicing getting into and out of so that I could be as quick and quiet as possible when I needed to hide, which was often. I was always on the alert, even when happily playing house with my dolls. The consequences were much too severe not to be.

It wasn't until elementary school that I began to realize my life at home was not normal. My classmates did not need to hide to stay safe. They were never awakened in the middle of the night by the sounds of screaming voices and chairs hitting walls. They did not lie on their bedroom floors peering through the gaps under their doors, watching for approaching feet that would soon make their way inside. They did not wake up morning after morning to see new holes in walls and doors that weren't there the night before, holes made by angry fists. Although I loved elementary school, it was there I realized I was different. My classmates were not afraid to go home. It was also there that I found the name for my fears: alcoholism.

My dad had been an alcoholic since well before I was born. I never knew my dad when he was sober. While I rarely saw him drink more than a beer or two at a time, I began putting the pieces together as I grew up. He liked working late and going out to do random "errands." He hid for long periods of time in the garage and, if all else failed, created a fight so he could storm out of the house to drink. He was an angry, unpredictable, and violent man who had an obsession with the female body and a propensity to always play the victim. Our house was a chaotic and scary environment where no one was safe from his abuse. Although I loved my dad dearly, I was terrified of him.

If you were to ask any of my teachers from elementary through high school, I was a high-achieving and hardworking student with a bright and successful future ahead of me. I loved school. It was my safe place where I felt loved and cared for. I wanted nothing more than to please my teachers. I always earned straight A's, mastered new assignments quickly, and volunteered for anything that needed to be done. I came in early and stayed late to help out as needed. I adored my teachers and even dreamed that they'd take me home with them. My mom eventually left my dad, remarried, and moved us across the country. This confirmed for my dad his identity as a victim, sending him deeper into a spiral of alcohol and drugs. He became more erratic, more inappropriate, and volatile. Spending vacations and holidays with him became increasingly difficult. I never knew exactly what to expect, but I always knew I would not escape unharmed. I began dreading those visits, particularly after puberty when his focus on my body intensified.

I was always a quiet and compliant child. I wanted to please everyone, and I did what I was told. An internal battle raged inside me when, as a teenager, I began wanting to say no to my dad. I struggled with this new desire to stand up for myself. I knew this wasn't typical teenage rebellion, but rather a natural inclination to protect myself. The trouble was I had no voice. I didn't have the ability to say no to anyone, much less my father, who terrified me. But even if I had a voice, it would not have mattered. It was an unequal match between a full-grown man, whose anger was fueled by decades of mental illness and reality-altering substances, and a powerless child who desperately wanted to be loved by her father and feared his wrath.

I had already witnessed what happened when someone tried to stand up to my dad. It never ended well. Speaking out never helped; instead, I learned the best way to get through it was to be quiet. This lesson was reinforced every time I remembered watching my dad dropkick my brother after he attempted to stand up to my dad and protect my mom.

My dad died from cirrhosis of the liver when I was a senior in high school. He died jobless, underweight, and completely alone. In fact, it was several days before someone found him dead on his kitchen floor. I wept and my heart broke for him, despite the years of abuse I had endured. It was what counselors call "complicated grief." And my life certainly became more complicated after my dad died. Not only was he my parent, but he was also the reason I had spent my life in survival mode. Now the enemy was gone and the war was over. It should have been time to relax in the peace of knowing I was safe from any further torment. Instead, I came completely undone.

My deterioration did not happen overnight. I had already been struggling with some depression and body image issues before my dad's death. But after he died, a lifetime of memories full of fear and abuse began overwhelming me like tidal waves—one after another. My need to be in survival mode ended, and I was left with nothing but my raw emotions and vivid memories.

I struggled with insomnia. When I was able to sleep, I woke from intense nightmares drenched in sweat. I couldn't concentrate or sit still and jumped at any sudden noise or movement. I stopped eating almost altogether and obsessed about how fat I thought I was. I was withdrawn, unhappy, and spent enormous amounts of time contemplating suicide. What bothered me the most was that I couldn't get my brain to turn off. The spinning chaos in my head never ended. It was always increasing, never giving me a moment of peace. I was desperate for relief. I wanted to escape.

I don't know how I got the idea, I had never heard of it. But one night it came to me with such clarity that I didn't even pause to question it. That night I began cutting. I found an X-ACTO knife in the house that was used for various crafting and home-improvement projects and hid it in my nightstand. I began slashing my wrists and arms on a daily basis, each time getting bolder and cutting deeper. Despite the increasing amount of blood that would pour out, I felt very little pain. And that is exactly why I cut. For those few moments when I was running a razor blade across my flesh, my brain slowed down. For those moments the spinning chaos stopped, and the *only* things I thought about were the razor, my arm, and the blood. That was the closest thing to relief I could find.

I remember the night I fell apart—the night I could no longer keep going. Until then, although I was quickly spiraling down into a dark abyss, I continued functioning on a high level. I maintained my 4.0 GPA taking numerous advanced placement courses with a lot of homework and continued training as a competitive gymnast for as many as four hours a day. I also taught gymnastics classes for preschool and school-aged children to offset the fees for my own training.

I'm not sure anyone could have foreseen what occurred next. One day I lay down on my bedroom floor, stared blankly at the wall, and didn't get up. I actually couldn't get up—even if I had found one remaining cell in my body that wanted to. I was done. There was nothing left in me. That day I stopped going to school and stopped going to my gymnastics team practices. In seemingly a split second I went from going one hundred miles per hour to zero. I was an empty and broken lump on my bedroom floor without any hope. I eventually did pick myself up off the floor . . . to write a suicide note.

It wasn't long before I was hospitalized for the first time. I was actually excited to be hospitalized. I thought it would be a peaceful place of rest and healing, where I would be kept safe from myself and doctors would make me better.

What I got was a hallway full of locked doors, twelve angry, psychotic adolescents, and a few tired staff members whose main concern was making sure patients did not disrupt their day. I had to fend off inappropriate male patients, dodge laundry baskets being hurled down the hallway in protest, endure staff comments about how much I ate, and was given way more medication than attention and eye contact from doctors. I left there with a paper bag full of medications and absolutely no healing. But I did learn one thing from that psychiatric unit: I learned how to make myself throw up.

The next years are what my family jokingly calls "the dark years." I was consumed with depression, post-traumatic stress disorder, and anorexia. My life became centered around doctors, therapy, and medication, and I spent years in hospitals. When I say years, I am not exaggerating. I found myself in a seemingly endless cycle of hospitals where I would be kept for eight or nine months and then transferred to another when doctors didn't know what else to do. I was consistently transferred back and forth between hospitals specializing in eating disorders and hospitals specializing in trauma. One would keep me for a period of time and, when I didn't improve, said it was because of the other diagnosis, and I'd be promptly sent to a different hospital.

I went through inpatient, residential, partial hospitalization, and intensive outpatient services in some of the "best" programs in the country. I was locked up, medicated, and fed through a feeding tube. I talked in groups, journaled, drew pictures, and hit chairs with foam bats to get my anger out. I cried for days at a time, tried to tell all my "secrets," and walked around in shoes without laces. Still I remained completely and utterly broken—only now I was strapped with hundreds of thousands of dollars in hospital bills.

There are many things I would like to forget about those years in hospitals. I would like to forget the drowsiness I felt from being given handfuls of medications at a time and then my sense of injustice when staff yelled at me for falling asleep in group therapy. I would like to forget the doctor who told me I was like an abused and scared horse that he would tame by holding me down until I stopped fighting. I would like to forget being forcibly picked up by staff members, stripped, and put in a seclusion room with padded walls simply because my crying was disruptive. I would like to forget the nurses who lectured me about how "the past is the past" and how I needed to "grow up and get over it."

I would like to forget about the time I overheard staff talking about me but no one could remember my name. Most of all I would like to forget knowing I was viewed as nothing more than an annoying patient filling a hospital bed, who could be ignored simply because I was mentally ill.

After about five long years of various hospitalizations, I was at a residential (long-term) treatment center, and I remember being called in to see my doctor. At this point I had been placed on more than two dozen medications in various combinations and was being fed primarily through a feeding tube surgically inserted into my stomach. Whatever progress I made was never enough to give my treatment team hope that I would succeed once discharged.

I entered my doctor's office and sat in the fancy leather chair across from where he sat at his massive oak desk. He proceeded to tell me that I was hopeless. He had done everything he could, there was nothing else he could do, and I would likely be institutionalized for life. I remember watching his mouth move as he told me I would always need medication and hospitalization. Although he thought I might be able to leave this particular hospital someday, I would spend the rest of my life needing frequent "tune-ups" in residential or inpatient facilities and it was doubtful that I would ever hold a job. In other words, my future was nonexistent. As I stumbled out of that doctor's office in a state of shock, my brain began working overtime to understand what I had just been told.

Once I wrapped my head around what the doctor laid out for me, I was determined to find another future. I came up with a plan of my own: suicide. I decided I would rather die than live the rest of my life as a hospital patient being tormented by my past. As a veteran of hospitals, it was not difficult to devise a plan for taking my own life while still being locked down and constantly supervised. As much as institutions and staff do to prevent patients from harming themselves, there is always a way if you are determined. And I had a lot of willpower concerning my future at this point. Before I could do anything, however, something stopped me. I don't know exactly what. I just know that suddenly my plan didn't sound good to me. But neither did my doctor's plan. Unfortunately I didn't have a third option. *Yet.*

It was around this time a few specific people were placed in my path. Looking back, I know it was God who placed these people in my life. I just had no idea who He was at the time. I did not grow up in a Christian home, nor had I ever been to church. I had no idea who Jesus was, and the few pictures I saw of Him, bloody and hanging from a cross with nails through His hands and feet, gave me nightmares. In fact, growing up, I was rather irritated when people tried to preach to me, quote scriptures at me, or look at me with sad eyes and tell me they were "praying for me to be saved." Despite this, in that hospital God was pursuing me in His gentle and patient way so that I might come to know Him.

I have to admit something. The first time I went to church, I did not go for God. I went for Diet Coke. Diet Coke was one of the many things I was not allowed to have while in hospitals. It was one of the things I missed and craved the most. While hospitals could deny me Diet Coke, however, they could not legally deny my right to attend church.

When a fellow hospital patient invited me to attend church with her on Sundays, I turned her down. Week after week she'd ask, and week after week I'd say no. Finally, one week she asked me again, but before I could say no, she told me there was a Diet Coke machine in the lobby. I went to church every week after that and sat in the lobby drinking can after can of Diet Coke. But while I drank, the church service was being piped through speakers into the lobby. The worship music began to capture me. I adored the idea of God loving me as His precious daughter and felt my heart leap when I heard about finding freedom and serenity in Christ.

The music is why I started putting down my Diet Cokes and wandering into the back of the main sanctuary. The music is why I ended up in the church service the day I first heard Jeremiah 29:11: "'For I know the plans I have for you,' declares the Lord, 'plans to prosper you and not to harm you, plans to give you hope and a future" [NIV]. Until then, my only options were my doctor's plan for my future and my plan to end my life. This scripture gave me my third option.

Around this time I became good friends with another patient in the hospital. She was in the process of applying to Mercy Ministries. I watched her walk through the application process and was excited for her when she got accepted, but I wasn't sure about this Mercy place. I mean it was *all* about God. The schedule revolved around Bible study, classes, and worship. I hadn't sat through an entire one-hour church service on Sunday yet! As ridiculous as the thought sounded to me, there was something in my heart that wanted to go to Mercy. There was something in my heart that wanted God.

I didn't tell anyone when I started filling out the application to Mercy. This was mostly because I couldn't explain it logically—to myself or anyone else. I had three options: a lifetime of medication and hospitals (my doctor's plan), suicide (my plan), or go to Mercy to get healed by God (God's plan). I chose the third plan because I strongly disliked plans one and two, not because I knew God was the answer. But my reasons weren't important. God had a plan. But in my mind if this God-thing didn't work, I'd go with plan two.

Now Mercy was my new goal—I needed to get there. But Mercy is just one place God uses to show His love and healing power. He did not wait until I was at Mercy to begin showing Himself to me. He began transforming me immediately—in a hospital while being tube-fed, overmedicated, and kept within locked halls. I began reading about God, completing assignments that were part of the Mercy application process. I got my first Bible, a children's Bible with lots of pictures. I read about Noah and Jonah for the first time.

I also sat in church on Sundays for the entire service and only drank my Diet Coke before and after. One Sunday the pastor began talking about how much God loves us and wants us to know Him. He talked about how precious we are to God and the freedom and joy that come from knowing Him. He talked about the sacrifice God made so that we could know Him, and how His Son Jesus took our sins and made us pure and clean. That all sounded really good to me. The pastor then asked if there was anyone in the audience who did not have a personal relationship with Christ but wanted to accept Him into their heart and know Him. I stood up. That was the day I accepted Jesus as my Lord and Savior.

I came to Mercy in January 2004. I got on the airplane by myself and was terrified about what was on the other end. I desperately wanted Mercy to be different from all the other hospitals and treatment centers I had been in, but I had my doubts. And I had only just begun my journey with God—maybe I was getting in way over my head. As a Mercy staff member drove me from the airport to the Mercy home, the radio was playing. It was set to a local Christian station. Just when I thought my anxiety would make me leap out of the moving car and run back to the airport, a song came on the radio. It was one of my favorite worship songs among the small handful I knew at that point. An overwhelming peace came over me, and I knew I was exactly where I needed to be. That song, "I Can Only Imagine," was confirmation it was all going to be OK.

Mercy was like a spiritual boot camp filled with the raw emotions of brokenness interrupted by moments of glorious healing and restoration. It was full of Bible studies, worship, and spiritual teachings. It was also full of cooking, cleaning, and learning to get along with thirty-nine other girls wrestling with the demons of their past and trying to grant God control. There was intense laughter and seemingly endless tears, all within a place that radiated nothing but love. It was nothing like the hospitals I was used to.

Something amazing happens when you bring God into the middle of your pain and ask Him to heal it: He does. Completely. This was perhaps the most profound difference about the counseling at Mercy. God is the center. In previous therapy I was used to talking and crying about the painful parts of my past. That usually only left me emotionally raw and exhausted, with nothing actually changed. At Mercy, God is the ultimate counselor, and because of who He is, He can actually heal.

One phenomenal thing I learned about God is how I am unique and precious to Him. He cares for me as an individual, not as one girl in a crowd of others. Because of this, His way of healing is unique and personal. How He joins me in my pain and heals my hurts is different from how He does it for anyone else. This became apparent to me during one particular counseling session. I had told my counselor about all the messages I received from my dad and still carried with me. Messages that I was unlovable, spiteful, selfish, cold, worthless, hurtful, and hateful. I was in tears as I recited all the things I believed about myself. Then my counselor prayed for God to come into the center of it. I closed my eyes, still a bit skeptical about the process.

It turns out God doesn't need 100 percent belief and faith in order to work. He only needs a little. With my eyes closed, I suddenly saw an image with such clarity that I knew it was not one from me; it was from God. In this vision, a pair of hands reached from the side holding out my most beloved Cabbage Patch doll, Angelique, for me to take. Angelique was my tiniest baby doll, the one that I cared for, protected, and loved dearly. There was no audible voice, but I heard the message loud and clear. It was God saying:

> *My precious child. Those messages you heard growing up are not who you are. They are lies. When you take care of your baby doll, that reflects who you are. You are tender, caring, protective, and nurturing. You are gentle, kind, and loving. That is your heart. That is who you are. I know because I created you.*

When I opened my eyes, they overflowed with tears of inexplicable joy. I'd just experienced God healing some deep wounds I never thought would heal.

During my time at Mercy, I developed a deeper relationship with Christ. I learned more about who He is, who I am in Him, and how beautiful I am to Him. I experienced a tremendous amount of healing, found a voice, and, for the first time ever, knew that I had value and worth simply because I am a daughter of the King. To me this is what it means to be transformed by Christ.

I graduated from Mercy in August 2004 healthy and whole, ready to walk out all I had learned. I knew it wouldn't be easy; I was leaving the safe walls of Mercy to enter a world full of stress, temptation, and sin. But that is where God calls us—into the world. I knew I needed to stay focused on God and remember the four "stay-ins": stay in prayer, stay in the Word, stay in church, and stay in fellowship with other believers.

It was the last two stay-ins that led me to move to Nashville. At least there I knew where to attend church and have relationships with other believers. Although I had never imagined living in Nashville, I knew it was where I was meant to be. I flew home, packed up my little Honda Civic with all I owned, and headed toward Tennessee. Little did I know that Tennessee would truly become home to me.

Once in Tennessee I found a place to live and took a job as a nanny for two families who each recently had their first child. Not only did I enjoy caring for two of the sweetest babies ever, I also saw two examples of loving Christian families. These families have both had more children, and I am still part of their lives. I am at every birthday party, attend school plays, go on family vacations, and am on the sideline cheering for various soccer, baseball, and hockey games. My eldest "baby" is now in third grade, and I am delighted by the privilege of being considered family.

In addition to working as a nanny, I took courses at a local state university to get my college degree. I graduated in 2006 with a bachelor's degree in psychology and was awarded highest honors. After graduation I was accepted into Vanderbilt University's doctoral program in quantitative psychology. I was trained as an applied researcher in children and adolescent mental health and learned advanced statistical techniques for large research projects funded by the National Institute of Mental Health and the Department of Defense. I earned the title of "doctor" when I graduated with my PhD in May 2013.

I hope to use my training to work with Christian ministries and nonprofits to demonstrate their effectiveness and develop ways to improve upon them. For example, I have a passion for "transitional youth"—young people who are leaving a structured environment such as Mercy or even foster care settings. It is my belief that individuals are more successful in this transition when they have certain supports and resources.

Above all, I would like to use my skills and training to apply quantitative measures to prove the success rate of programs such as Mercy Ministries and demonstrate the connection between faith and healing.

During this journey I also met and fell in love with an amazing Christian man. He is sweet, caring, and funny, always knowing how to make me laugh. He adores me and tells me this multiple times a day. He thinks I am precious and beautiful and treats me wonderfully. We were married in 2012 and look forward to the rest of our lives together, including starting a family. Having children has been a desire of my heart for as long as I can remember; plus, God already showed me that He created me with the qualities that will make me a great mom.

People often ask if it is hard to share the details of my past, particularly the disturbing details of my life before Mercy. I can tell you that it is not. That is how God is. When He heals, He heals completely. There are no Band-Aids or temporary fixes that leave wounds to be ripped open again in the future. God's healing is complete and permanent. Therefore it is not difficult to share my story. That's not to say that Satan does not try to use my past against me and make me stumble—he does. But I can laugh at his feeble attempts because he has already lost. My God has already conquered it all!

The doctors were wrong about me. Today I am healthy, happy, and enjoying my life. I have hope and excitement for the future, and peace in the moment. I am a wife, sister, friend, and, most importantly, a child of God. I have a prosperous and hopeful future that God ordained. I am proof that God will use anything to draw people to Him—even Diet Coke.

CHAPTER EIGHT

Heart of the Matter

As you read about Michele, what were you thinking? Were you scratching your head, overwhelmed with pain for Michele, and shouting into the pages of this book saying something like, "Just eat something, Michele! Just stop cutting! Just trust in God; you'll feel so much better if you do!" These are the comments we at Mercy hear all the time from onlookers who don't understand why people cut and starve themselves.

I understand your confusion. But if it were as simple as telling someone what to do, we wouldn't have girls spending thousands and thousands of dollars and sometimes years of time in rehab facilities only to end up back at square one before they come to us at Mercy. Some of the finest facilities in the country charge as much as two thousand dollars per day in hopes of helping these women, but their success rate is very low.

Eating disorders and cutting are not easy to overcome, but God promises that "in all these things we are more than conquerors through Him who loved us" (Rom. 8:37). In Christ we *are* overcomers.

The whys behind Michele's behavior are easy to understand if we explore beneath the surface. Cutting was her way of temporarily expressing and releasing her pain. Michele said, "I was desperate for relief from a lifetime of memories." Cutting was her escape, if only for a few minutes. Michele only felt a temporary relief when she cut, so she cut more and more, thus beginning an increasingly destructive cycle. The more often she gave in to the urge to harm herself, the more often she felt the urge.

Michele's self-harm began when she felt the pain in her life controlled her. She said, "As a young girl I was compliant and quiet, never standing up to my dad. I never had a voice." Cutting became her voice, and she could decide when and how to use it.

Like Michele, people often self-harm to communicate feelings and emotions they don't know how to verbalize, feelings including anxiety, fear, loneliness, nervousness, and anger. Often they are trying to reduce the intensity of these emotions or avoid them altogether. Many times they have experienced severe sexual abuse during childhood that later results in cutting. Sadly this was the case with Michele. As everything in her life was so chaotic, she utilized cutting as something she could control.

Self-harm is a secretive behavior and often goes undetected. Michele maintained a 4.0 GPA, took accelerated program classes, and taught gymnastics, all while she was cutting in secret. Michele used self-harm to simply escape from reality. People also use self-harm to cope with stressful and discouraging events.

Shame and depression are two other emotions closely associated with cutting. Shame makes a person believe they deserve to be punished. "You are worthless," was Michele's mantra. Depression made her believe she had no way out and that things would never change.

Understanding the depth of Michele's despair gives me a heart for people who cut. Self-harm is the outward expression of pain and hurt hidden deep within. The emotional pain is so overwhelming that people cut to relieve the inner pain, but the hurt is still there when the outward pain is gone. The relief, then, is only temporary.

It is so important that we don't ignore this tragedy. It affects so many people. Kim Gratz, director of personality disorders research at the University of Mississippi Medical Center, says "it's hard to gauge the prevalence of this behavior…[but] studies find that between 17 and 40 percent of college students admit to committing self harm and between 15 and 30 percent of high school students do."[1]

People have practiced cutting as a means of desperate

expression since before 540 BC. Scripture refers to it in 1 Kings 18:28. Elijah challenged four hundred fifty prophets of Baal to pray to their feeble gods, knowing that Yahweh was the only able, true, and loving God. When Baal's prophets' prayers went unanswered, the prophets became desperate, raving and cutting themselves with their swords in frustration and shame.

Elijah called upon the living God to show Himself strong and true among the people (v. 30). What happened next was a demonstration that left no doubt as to God's power and might. Elijah built an altar unto the Lord and even drenched it with water. Then, when Elijah called on the name of the Lord, fire fell and consumed the burnt offering and dried up the water. All who witnessed this miracle fell on their faces and said, "The LORD, He is God!" (v. 39). If only Baal's prophets had called upon the true God! That's whom we point to at Mercy: the one true God. When a girl decides to call upon Yahweh, He steps in for her just as He did for Elijah. Frustration and shame are then replaced with relief, love, and healing.

Michele said it best: "Something amazing happens when you bring God into the middle of your pain and ask Him to heal it—He does, completely. This was perhaps the most profound difference about the counseling at Mercy. God is the center."

At Mercy, girls who have struggled with cutting learn to ask God to heal the broken places in their hearts by first asking God's only Son to live inside their hearts. They give up control and forgive others, themselves, and God. They "take captive" thoughts of self-harm and replace ungodly beliefs with godly ones. Here is an example of one young woman's thought process.

She came through our Mercy program and overcame her issue of cutting by replacing lies with truths.

- **Ungodly belief:** I need to self-injure in order to feel release from my pain.

- **Godly belief:** God is my source of healing and strength. I choose to rely on Him to help me through anything I encounter. As I give Him my pain, He will give me the release I need through His peace and healing. I can trust Him to be faithful.

There is something very powerful about replacing the lies we believe about ourselves with the truth of what God's Word says about us. This is an exercise that the girls who come through our program do with the help of their counselors. Over the years hundreds of these girls have been completely set free from the need to cut as a result of being able to change the way they think and what they believe about themselves.

Michele also struggled with a severe eating disorder. While the outward signs of an eating disorder may seem drastically different from self-harm behavior, the underlying issues—the whys—of eating disorders are strikingly similar to the whys of cutting. Often these two issues are playing out simultaneously in a girl's life when she arrives at Mercy. Suicidal tendencies, chronic depression, and many other issues may be present as well. There are several types of eating disorders, and severe and sometimes permanent damage can result from any of them. Statistics say one in five young women struggles with an eating disorder.[2] Eating disorders often go undetected due to their secretive nature.

Outside influences such as the media, movies, TV, magazines, and the Internet play a role in eating disorders. But that does not mean we should isolate ourselves from today's culture. It is important to understand how outside influences can affect us. The fashion industry is filled with girls engaged in a dangerous competition over who can be the thinnest, prettiest, and sexiest. Most, if not all, of the photos you see on advertisements, covers of magazines, and billboards are extensively retouched. The bodies and faces represented in most of these photos are not even humanly possible!

Although the media, the fashion industry, and even family abuse can influence an eating disorder, more than likely they were not the prime instigators. Most eating disorders stem from deep emotional, psychological, and spiritual roots. Just as in Michele's life, not eating was a way for her to avoid unpleasant emotions and feelings.

Michele and other girls who struggle with an intense fear of gaining weight, perfectionism, and distorted body image are simply struggling with other forms of self-harm and self-hate. Just as in the case where a girl has struggled with cutting, girls who come to Mercy who are struggling with eating disorders have to take captive the thoughts that lead to eating disorder behavior and replace ungodly beliefs with godly ones.

Here is another example:

- **Ungodly belief:** I can never meet the standard. I can never be thin enough or perfect enough for others to love me.

- **Godly belief:** I am fully loved, completely accepted, and totally pleasing to God. I choose to surrender to Him, trusting my faith in Him and His ability to sustain me. I will seek to please God and not other people.

Before Mercy, Michele described herself as an "overmedicated, depressed, and anorexic mental patient whom doctors called hopeless." They told her that her future was bleak and she'd need continual "tune-ups," meaning she would be in and out of inpatient facilities for the rest of her life. They also said she would likely never be able to hold a job.

Michele has earned a PhD from Vanderbilt, is married to a Christian man, and is walking in freedom. How was this possible?

Michele represents thousands of young women who have reached out to Mercy Ministries for help since 1983. More often than not these young women have been in multiple treatment programs, including psychiatric facilities, and frequently been hospitalized, including hospitals that specialize in treating eating disorders. Unfortunately we have met many girls like Michele, who were told after going through all the various treatments that there was no hope. One thing I know is that people can argue about principles, but no one can argue with a hopeless life that has been utterly transformed.

In 2005 the chief of staff at one of the nation's elite inpatient eating disorder programs contacted me. This doctor wanted to visit our Nashville headquarters to meet with me, along with our program director and our director of counseling services. Though surprised, I eagerly agreed to meet with this renowned expert in eating disorders. For the sake of anonymity, let's call him Dr. Smith.

I will never forget the day that Dr. Smith came to Nashville and toured our international headquarters and our program facility that houses forty women. Dr. Smith was extremely complimentary about the excellence of our program. After the tour Dr. Smith and two of my leading staff members joined me in my office. We quickly learned the purpose of his visit.

Dr. Smith explained that he had noticed the great changes that had taken place in the lives of many of his former patients after they had been through our program at Mercy. He said he obviously cared about his patients and otherwise would not be doing what he was doing. It seemed to him that we were achieving much better results in our program than in the treatment program that he runs. He was wondering exactly what it was that we were doing to get such great results so that he could perhaps learn something that would improve the results of his program.

I sat stunned by what I was hearing. This was the first time any person from a secular treatment program had visited us and acknowledged that we were having amazing success with the young women we serve. In our earlier phone conversation Dr. Smith made it clear that he knew Mercy was a Christian program and that he was not a Christian. I had silently prayed God would help me to explain what was different about our program. "After all," I thought, "at least he respects us enough that he came out of his way to meet with us and ask questions."

In the simplest way I knew, I explained to Dr. Smith the heart of the Christian message: there is a way you can be forgiven for past mistakes, you can forgive the people who have hurt you, you can have the shame and guilt and condemnation lifted off of you, and you can receive healing for the pain and hurt of the past. I explained that only through Christ can a person receive a new heart and new spirit and realize that her past does not have to destroy her future.

Although Dr. Smith was respectful and attentive, it was clear that he could not fully comprehend what I was saying. Spiritual things have to be spiritually discerned. God's Word says the natural man cannot comprehend the things of God (1 Cor. 2:14). After an hour or so Dr. Smith shook hands with us and thanked us for our time. That was the last time I heard from him.

The takeaway from this experience for me was that I totally respect any person who will take time to seek out answers. The problem was that because he had never experienced what I was trying to share, he could not understand what I was saying.

Even though there has never been anyone else from a secular treatment program to visit our facilities since that time, we began receiving referrals from secular treatment programs when insurance money runs out or girls have reached the end of their stays and are still very sick. We welcome these referrals because we know that God has the power to transform any life—every life.

Let me share with you a great example of the power of a transformed life with words from a 2011 Mercy graduate from our California home:

> My doctor, whom I've seen for the last five or six years and who isn't a Christian, just called me. Before I came to Mercy, he had seen me at rock bottom and had said there was little—if any—hope for me. But today he called to ask me about Mercy Ministries so he could recommend the program to one of his [other] patients. Because of the change he noticed in my life during my last appointment, he was beside himself! He has seen that there is something different about Mercy.

The difference this doctor saw in his patient after her time at Mercy was the completed work of the Great Physician.

Chapter Nine

Fallen Towers

O N September 11, 2001, planes crashed into the World Trade Center, leaving more than one hundred unborn children to survive their fathers. They were left behind and now faced uncertainty, shrouded in loss and grief. We will never fully understand the weight of the emotional assault heaped upon these women as they prepared to bring their unborn babies into this world.

On 9/11 the bodies of the fathers of those unborn children lay silently below the fallen Twin Towers. God continued to carefully form their sons and daughters in the womb. In secret God planned each day of these children's lives, weaving hope, health, and purpose into each of them. He wept with each mother for her lost husband and held her close. God didn't allow His plans for them to fall into the rubble remaining of the Twin Towers.

While the world's eyes were fixed on the desolation left by 9/11, God began working in another young mother and the unborn baby boy she carried.

Meet Kathryne and her son Jackson, whose name means "the son of God's grace."

As I sit here and watch my husband read to my sweet wiggle-worm eighteen-month-old, it's hard to believe what path I was following thirteen years ago. As a senior in high school, I was carefree. Like any typical high schooler, I was not necessarily thinking about my future and was just living day to day for myself. I would say that I faced some of the typical struggles of that age: body image issues, insecurity, peer pressure, relationships gone bad, and rejection. I dabbled with drinking and partying, but being a basketball player helped keep that from becoming a regular part of my life.

Then I found out that my boyfriend had been lying to me about everything as well as cheating on me. This was the same person who had contributed to my body image issues leading me to restrict my food intake. I believed that I was not good enough and because I did not think I deserved better, I went back to him time and time again.

When I finally had enough, that's when I started spending lots of time with my friend Jackson. He was very special, and he made me feel special. What began with friendship eventually became more, and we both wondered if we might be destined for marriage one day—but college came first, and we chose to go to different schools.

As an average basketball player who thought she had to prove herself, I worked tirelessly to improve my shooting skills and my endurance. I was ready to show everyone that I could play, and I did—for about two minutes. It was the last scrimmage before regular season. I started the game as center and scored the first four points of the game. As I ran down the court full of adrenaline to score another two, I impulsively jump stopped and shot the ball to allow the opponent to run past me. As I landed, I heard a loud pop and fell to the floor curling my leg to my chest. Was this really happening? Yes—I had blown out my knee.

All my hard work apparently had been for nothing, and the disappointment of not being able to show everyone that I was really good was devastating. I was so determined to prove myself that I rehabbed my knee and put off surgery in order to try and play the last half of the season—but God had different plans. The practice before the game, I hurt my knee to the point that it was literally locked in a bent position. I felt out of control and once again was overwhelmed with disappointment. God later showed me that I did not need to prove myself and that my worth was not in my ability to play basketball or in anything else that I thought I could find worth in. At that time I was far from understanding this.

Along with these challenges at school, I had a father who drank, worked, and drank some more. I was so ready to be out from under his roof that I took one main thing into consideration when looking for colleges—distance! When I found a school that was far enough away to make a weekend visit practically out of the question—not to mention by the beach—I was sold. What I did not think about was that I would be far away from everyone else I loved too.

One week before moving away for college, I experienced one of the most painful times of my life. Jackson, the man I thought I might marry one day, was killed in a tragic car accident. I was torn apart—it was a sadness unlike anything I had ever imagined. I was confused. Why him? He was the "good kid" whom everyone liked. I replayed over and over the last time we hung out together. What I had said and what I had *not* said. There was regret that brought new meaning to the word. Nothing could be undone or redone.

Attending Jackson's funeral and then leaving to enter College of Charleston a few days later left me in a grief-stricken whirlwind. As I arrived and began to get settled into my freshman year of college, deep sadness continued to plague me. I cried out and questioned God, but I didn't really want an answer—I just wanted to wallow in my tears.

Desperate to fill the void I felt from losing Jackson, it didn't take long until I found someone to cling to. I latched on to the first guy who showed me some attention and quickly found myself in an emotionally dependent relationship. I was lonely and looking for love wherever I could find it. We became sexually active, and coed dorms made it easy to continue in that lifestyle. But deep down I knew I needed to end this relationship. Before the end of my freshman year, I decided to move back home because I recognized that I was not healthy and needed more support.

I discovered I was pregnant the week after moving back home. Telling my parents was an awful experience. My mom could barely look at me, and my dad was so hurt that he couldn't even talk—at first anyway. After a few drinks he had quite a few choice words for me—words that I cannot repeat. To put it mildly, he told me that my life was over; I had screwed up so badly that it couldn't be fixed.

My father was embarrassed and said something like "I'm just disappointed you got caught." What? So, did that mean he wasn't disappointed in the fact I was having sex outside of marriage? Well, one thing was for sure, he did not want me to tell anyone. I was a disgrace and we would just have to get rid of "the problem." I knew in my heart that abortion was wrong and that I was not willing to follow that plan. I was fearful, though, that somehow he could force me to have an abortion. I mean, what other choice did I have? It's not as if I could afford to get my own place and raise a baby by myself. It was becoming clear that I would not be able to live at home and raise a baby, so I didn't know what options were left.

In my teenage mind the best thing to do was to run away to my boyfriend's house. His parents were nice, so surely they would help us out. Bags packed with everything I had of any worth (so I could pawn things for money), I was ready to go. Luckily, my mom hunted me down before I could get out of town. Although she was disappointed too, she was my mom and she loved me. She knew I needed her support. My mom told me that abortion was not the only option. In her way she was offering her approval of my decision to have this baby. A few weeks later my mom told me about Mercy Ministries. Even with limited information, anywhere would have been better than home. Living in the same house as my disapproving father was unbearable.

I walked through the doors of Mercy Ministries on September 11, 2001. As if I wasn't already fearful enough, the terrorist attacks on America added to the shock of the morning. It was difficult when my mom and sister left. I was so sad and once again felt completely alone.

Although I felt alone, it did not take long for me to realize that wasn't true. Clearly I was not alone, since there were thirty-nine other girls living there with me. Also, the staff was so kindhearted and compassionate. They were obviously filled with God's love, which was something I had only experienced in small doses in the past. My experience at Mercy was life altering! I thought I was coming to Mercy to escape the ridicule and disdain of my father and to deal with my pregnancy, but I received so much more. I received God's grace. I made a commitment to live for Christ and received a new beginning through God's gift of forgiveness.

When I came to Mercy I was still undecided about what I wanted to do with my baby. I thought I wanted to be a mom, but I was also considering adoption. Mercy educated me about these two options and supported me through the decision-making process. What I appreciate about Mercy is that they not only value babies' lives, but they also care so much about the mothers. Mercy does everything in its power to honor each woman's choice in deciding whether to raise the baby or adopt. Mercy understands the gravity of this type of decision, and I believe they honored me throughout my entire decision-making process.

Ultimately I chose to place my sweet baby boy up for adoption. Through a lot of prayer and counseling, I felt like this was what God wanted me to do. I knew that I wanted this baby to grow up with a father who was present. And there were other things I wanted for him that I could not provide on my own. I was involved in deciding about the adoptive family and how much contact we would have, and we talked about how this would affect my life. I am so thankful I was at Mercy during this significant season in my life. At home I would have walked in shame through my entire pregnancy.

At Mercy I learned that my baby was not a surprise to God. Although it certainly caught *me* off guard, my Father in heaven already knew about this child. I learned that His grace was sufficient—meaning that He was able to provide my needs and the needs of this child if I was willing to call out to Him and rely on Him. I learned all these things through the teaching and guidance at Mercy and through reading the Bible. Matthew 6:25–27 promised that God would provide for my needs, and Romans 8:1 said that He was not ashamed of me! I clung to God's Word and to its promises because they are *so* much better than what the world wants me to believe about myself.

In addition to adoption counseling, I was also receiving biblical counseling for all my other "junk." When I look back at my time in Mercy's program, I am grateful that I was able to set aside those months to address the past hurts in my life. Most people don't have the opportunity to call "time out" from real life to get things back in order. I recognize now that this was truly a gift from God. I was able to put life on hold to learn what it really means to live. God wants us to involve Him in our lives. I learned that life without a relationship with God is lonely and disappointing. But it is our choice to enter a relationship with God and to decide what importance we place on that relationship.

The more I learned about the Bible, the more I wanted to know. I began to read more and to pray more often. Learning how to be in relationship with my heavenly Father was one of the most significant aspects of my time at Mercy. As I actively pursued my relationship with God through prayer and conversation, praise and worship, and learning what Scripture says, I began to feel God's presence more than ever before. I began to feel less and less alone—not only because I experienced God's presence, but also because I experienced His love through the staff at Mercy. They really cared.

My counselor helped me work through significant issues, such as forgiving my dad for things he had said and done, as well as the things that he had not said or done but I wished he had. The restoration of my relationship with my dad was nothing short of a miracle. Each day I had to choose to walk in forgiveness rather than hold on to hurt. My counselor helped me forgive many other people and also to ask forgiveness for hurtful things I had done.

During my time at Mercy, God showed me that He is faithful. I will never question this. I can honestly say He is real. He is active in our lives to the extent we allow Him to be involved. It's so fun for me to look back and remember some of my prayers that He was faithful to answer. God answered such specific prayers that His involvement was undeniable. Probably the best example is the family He provided to adopt my son.

God had the perfect couple in mind to parent my precious little baby. They exceeded my list of requirements. This is one of the coolest things about Mercy—Mercy recognizes the importance of a birth mother's involvement in choosing a family for her child. And they don't want you to settle for less. After I examined the files of potential adoptive families, I found two that I felt were good possibilities, but I did not feel 100 percent certain that either were the right family for my son. Through what can only be described as a divine series of appointments, another couple heard about Mercy and decided to rush in their application. Mercy gave me their family book to look through just before I left on a weekend pass. That weekend my family and I looked through the book together. My brother-in-law recognized the potential adoptive mom and realized he had worked with her several years earlier. He remembered that she had been extremely kind. I was excited about this couple. They seemed to be exactly who I was looking for.

Mercy understands God's heart! They do not want us to compromise on the qualities we believe God is showing us when choosing our adoptive parents. After meeting this couple, I knew they were the family who would raise my baby. I had one main request: they name this little boy after my friend Jackson, who had died in the car accident. I had already asked Jackson's parents if that would be OK and they happily agreed. This might seem odd, but it also served as a sort of closure for me.

Fast-forward twelve years from that time in my life, and I am happy to say that I still have a close relationship with God. I am happily married, and we have a precious little girl. I have walked through many trials since graduating Mercy Ministries. Mercy and God don't promise that life will be easy or without struggles, but Mercy and God's Word taught me that I can get through anything with God's help.

I think we all probably remember exactly where we were on September 11, 2001, when the two planes flew into the Twin Towers. As Kathryne entered Mercy that day, she felt as though her life lay in ruins, much like those towers. Yet as Kathryne walked through the doors, she sensed there was hope for her future, without knowing how things would end up.

Although Kathryne initially thought she would parent her child, she was very much looking forward to going through the basic decision-making classes that Mercy provides for every pregnant young woman who walks through our doors. After studying the facts, considering the options, and earnestly praying, she felt adoption was the best decision. She could also bless a couple unable to have children on their own.

After Kathryne made her decision, a settled peace came over her heart. She knew she had made the very best choice for her life and for her child. She began meeting one-on-one with our director of adoptions, who oversees our licensed adoption agency. Kathryne provided what she wanted in an adoptive couple and was educated about the adoption process itself. Though this process was new to Kathryne, Mercy has been involved with hundreds of adoptions over the years. Our heart is to work with each girl to make sure the desires of her heart are met where her child is concerned.

Mercy was three years old in 1986 when we began taking in girls who were pregnant. Our age range was thirteen to twenty-eight. The first pregnant girl we took in was thirteen years old and knew that she was not ready to be a parent—she was still a child herself. It was at this point I began praying diligently for God to show me what He wanted us to do concerning the adoption process. I was confident we could help prepare a young girl who wanted to parent to be the very best parent she could be, but the adoption process was new to me.

God showed me very clearly that He wanted us to tell each pregnant girl who walked through our doors that she was loved by us and loved by God. He wanted us to tell her that we were proud of her for having the courage to carry her child to term, regardless of whether she chose to parent or place her child for adoption. We have always believed our job is to help a girl develop a relationship with God and be led by His Spirit so that she can pray and make her own decision. We have remained true to that principle.

In 1986 when I began seeking God about how to handle the adoption process—fully understanding the gravity of deciding who someone's parents would be—I was overwhelmed by the fact that God is God and I am not. How could a person like me, or any of my staff for that matter, be the one to decide who is going to raise a child? It was way too much for me to handle, so with tears streaming down my face, I hit my knees and cried out to God: "You have to show me how You want me to do this!" God showed me that if a young girl chooses to parent, we are to prepare her to be the very best parent she can be. If a girl chooses adoption, we are to honor her by helping her find an adoptive family who meets the desires of her heart. Each young girl who chooses adoption makes a list of everything she wants in an adoptive couple, and we assure her no detail is too small if it is important to her. One girl even put on her list that the family had to have a particular kind of dog, and we honored her request!

As Kathryne's son grew in her womb, the faith of God grew strong in her heart. She approached the adoption issue with the peace of God that passes all understanding and a strength of character that is not unfamiliar to me as girls grow in their personal relationships with Christ.

The day came when Kathryne was ready to make a list of what she wanted in an adoptive couple. She had spent so much time praying and was already excited to see what God was going to do. Immediately after she met with our director of adoptions, Kathryne came down the hall to my office to share her list with me. Bubbling with excitement, she handed me a piece of paper with the following qualities she was looking for: Christians who are adventurous, like to travel, love sports, live in the South, between the ages of twenty-seven and thirty-eight, married at least three years, who are close to their family and live in close proximity to them, who value education and would send him to college. It was exciting to see the peace Kathryne had and how solid she was in the decision to place her baby for adoption.

A couple of weeks later I was preparing to leave our facilities to head to the airport for a business trip to California. A Hollywood movie producer had contacted us about discussing the possibility of making a movie about Mercy Ministries. Just before I left, Kathryne came by my office again. She said, "I really want to ask you to pray for me because I found two couples out of all the couples who have applied at Mercy for adoption that I could be interested in. Even though both these couples meet the list of items I put together, I don't really feel a sense of peace that either one of them is right. Will I have any other choices?"

I replied that I would definitely pray for her. I explained about my trip and that I would return the following week and would be happy to talk with her when I had more time. I reiterated that she should not settle for anything less than what God had put in her heart for the adoptive couple and that she should never make a decision when she did not have peace about it. I promised Kathryne that God had the perfect parents for her child and that even if they were not in the files, we would find exactly who she was looking for. I reassured her that God would provide.

I left the office building and headed to the airport. This trip was filled with purpose. A movie about Mercy would bring awareness and support to our cause. But God had something even greater in mind—something that would impact lives and set unimaginable things in motion to astound many people, especially Kathryne and me.

In Los Angeles I drove to the restaurant where the business meeting was scheduled. The woman who was head of the production company was there to meet me. She quickly explained that she had brought her daughter along and that her daughter was pregnant. She thought it would be good for her daughter to meet me and hear about what I do. The first hour and a half we enjoyed a wonderful dinner and talked about the process of developing a movie, what it could mean for Mercy, and other details that seemed important at the time.

After a bit I began a conversation with the daughter about what we do at Mercy, about her life and whether she was planning to parent or place her baby for adoption. She told me that at first she had planned on adoption and had even chosen a couple but had since decided to parent her child, who was due in just a few weeks. I told her that interestingly enough the last conversation I had before leaving for the airport was with a young resident about her same age. The girl had completed her freshman year of college and discovered she was pregnant, and that her experience had been just the opposite. She came into the program thinking she was going to keep her baby, but after going through our basic decision-making process, she had decided on adoption.

This beautiful young girl made eye contact with her mom, looked back at me, and excitedly asked, "Has this girl chosen a couple?" I told her that no, not yet, but she had made a list of the qualities she was looking for in a couple. The daughter proceeded to tell me about the wonderful couple she had picked out. They lived in Dallas, Texas, and they were everything she had wanted in an adoptive couple. She hated that she had to disappoint them. They desperately wanted a child and had not been able to have one. I asked her to tell me more. She and her mother jumped in and began telling me how wonderful they were, and it didn't take long for me to figure out that everything they said about this couple was actually on Kathryne's list. I commented that it would probably be a good idea to connect me with this couple since they seemed so close to what Kathryne wanted. They agreed; we said good night and ended a very enjoyable evening.

The next morning I received a call from the movie producer. She asked if she could hook me into a three-way call with herself and the couple from Dallas. We talked for two hours without stopping!

That was the last time I talked to the movie producer and to date, no movie about Mercy has ever materialized. It was only the beginning, however, of my relationship with that couple. A few days later they overnighted me a book about their life, containing pictures of their immediate family, extended family, home, interests, the work they had done after graduating from the colleges they attended, and even the fact that the prospective adoptive father had played college baseball in South Carolina. It seemed surreal that everything on Kathryne's list fit exactly who this couple was. I made our director of adoptions aware, and we met with Kathryne to tell her the story of finding this couple and that they had sent their information for her consideration. Kathryne seemed interested in looking but said she wanted to be certain. I assured her that it did not matter to me whether this was the couple she chose and that it was her decision and nobody else's. She asked permission to take the book with her that weekend as she was going to visit her family and wanted to show them their profile... and the rest is history.

Kathryne asked that the couple fly to Nashville so they could meet face-to-face. She quickly fell in love with them. The final request she made before she said yes to selecting them was, as Kathryne has already shared, that they name the baby Jackson. They loved the name, and they also fell in love with Kathryne.

January 15, 2002, Jackson entered the world. Kathryne not only invited her family to be there for the birth, but she also invited the soon-to-be adoptive parents. Kathryne also decided to offer an invitation for Jackson's parents to visit the hospital to meet their late son's namesake, and they eagerly accepted. It was quite an emotional day—a day filled with joy and the feeling of full-circle restoration.

I can't explain what it was like for me that day. Kathryne asked her mother and me to witness Jackson's birth. What a special day that was!

Kathryne is one of the strongest young women I have ever

met. After giving birth, she returned to Mercy to go through the six weeks or so that we ask a girl to commit to after placing a baby for adoption. We want to make sure a girl is settled and at peace with her decision before graduating from Mercy. Kathryne made it through brilliantly and never once questioned her decision. Kathryne graduated in February 2002 and was excited about returning to College of Charleston that summer to finish her degree, which she received three years later.

After graduating, Kathryne took a job with the National Federation of Independent Business in Nashville, Tennessee, where she worked for a little more than two years. When Kathryne graduated from Mercy in 2002, we had no idea she would return in 2008 to work in our intake department. This department takes calls from young women all across the United States who are seeking help—young women just like Kathryne. At the time of this writing, Kathryne is not only still working at Mercy, but she has also received numerous promotions and is now the intake supervisor.

Kathryne married in 2008. She and her husband, Jon, had known each other for six years, three of which were spent dating. Jon and Kathryne have a little girl and intend to have more children in the future. Kathryne has remained extremely faithful in her walk with Christ.

God never ceases to amaze me how He orders our steps and directs our path for *His* purposes. What a God we serve that He would send me to Los Angeles to connect with a woman whom I would never see again, but who would connect me with a couple who would adopt a baby in answer to the prayers of a pregnant girl sitting in our Mercy home in Nashville.

That's the kind of God I want to know, and I hope you do too!

CHAPTER TEN

Choosing Forever

MERCY MINISTRIES HELPS people like Kathryne every day, but that wasn't always the case. As mentioned in a previous chapter, Mercy began taking in girls with unplanned pregnancies in 1986. Around this same time a Christian-based organization called Operation Rescue was just getting started and was addressing the issue of abortion head-on. There was unrest in the streets with people gathering at abortion clinics from both sides of the issue. Picketing often turned into fighting, bloodshed, and even killing in the name of saving lives.

And although I appreciated the passion and commitment of the pro-life movement, I found it difficult to find peace with some of the methods being used to fight abortion. God showed me my hypocrisy in speaking out against abortion while turning away pregnant girls. His message was very clear—I was to stop talking against abortion unless I was ready to obey Him and begin taking in unwed mothers!

But first we needed a building to house pregnant young women.

Wrong!

I prayed, "Give us a building and we'll start taking them in," and God's reply surprised me. He said, "You start taking them, and I'll give you the building."

This was the first time I felt God's heart for the unborn and their mothers. We'd been turning girls away for lack of space, but He was asking us not to wait another minute. The time to save lives was *now*. No pickets, no shouting or marching, no blocking abortion clinic doors—only doing what would save a life *today*.

The very next day I received a phone call from the pastor of a thirteen-year-old girl who was pregnant by her mother's thirty-seven-year-old boyfriend. Receiving this child-with-child into our program was both exciting and frightening, for the pain ran deep and the complexity of the situation was intimidating. While at Mercy this young mother found Christ and surrendered both her life and her baby to God. The infant was placed for adoption, and afterward God brought about healing and forgiveness between the girl and her mother. Restoration was achieved for everyone. Since then we've helped hundreds of girls the same way we did this first one.

To fight the injustice of abortion, Mercy has always felt the best defense is a good offense. Psalm 139 says it best: "Every life comes from God" (author paraphrase).

Scripture shows us that God has always given mankind the right to choose. If we look at Adam and Eve in the Garden of Eden, it was Eve's choice that brought about death, yet God loved Adam and Eve in spite of it.

People who are pro-abortion call themselves pro-choice, but the truth is that God is a God of choice, and our relationship with Him is based on our choosing to walk with Him—*or not*—every day. God showed me in 1986 that He wanted Mercy to provide a practical way for girls to choose life for their unborn babies. Deuteronomy 30:19 says: "This day I call heaven and the earth as witnesses against you that I have set before you life and death, blessings and curses. Now choose life, so that you and your children may live" (NIV).

We began accepting every young woman facing an unplanned pregnancy who called. When these girls arrive at Mercy, they are faced with yet another choice: whether to parent or to place their baby for adoption. We first educate the girls regarding the different challenges involved with both parenting and adoption. In addition to educating them, our job is to point the girls toward Christ and teach them to seek Him about His plans for their unborn children. Also, as with Kathryne in the previous chapter, we allow each mother who decides to place her baby for adoption the right to choose the adoptive parents, down to every last detail.

When God gave me the guidelines for Mercy's adoption agency and how it would look different from other programs, He showed me that we needed to remove all traces of fear and secrecy. When a couple is afraid to know facts about the birth mother and vice versa, the baby may find a home, but no one wins because the birth mother walks away with a hole in her soul and the adoptive parents live in fear that the mother might change her mind. Our focus at Mercy is to make sure that the young woman is totally healed and secure in her decision as she finishes the process of placing her child. We also want the adoptive parents to walk in peace for their future. "Fear has torment, but perfect love casts out all fear" (1 John 4:18, author's paraphrase).

As the expectant mother studies her choices for her baby's adoptive parents, she meets them, talks with them, and they pray together. After she chooses a couple, in each case the birth mother and the couple negotiate a mutual agreement about whether or not they will be present at the birthing in the hospital. Almost always the birth mother chooses to have an adoption placement ceremony during which the mother hands the baby over to the couple. By this time there's such a bond of love between everyone that all fear has lost its place and power in the situation. I've watched this process since our first adoption, and I know that God's ways are always higher and better than ours.

Obviously we began taking in pregnant girls without having

a new building, and we were bursting at the seams. Around that same time I was invited to speak at a weeklong evangelistic conference in Las Vegas. The meeting was wonderful, but by the time it was over I was exhausted. As I slipped into my seat on the plane, I closed my eyes and hoped for a few hours of peace.

"Excuse me."

I opened my eyes to see a medium-size man standing over me. He was wearing blue jeans, a T-shirt, and tennis shoes. I moved to let him squeeze by and hoped he wouldn't start talking to me. I was so tired all I wanted was to take a nap.

God had other plans. Even before he fastened his seat belt, he turned to me and asked, "So how much money did you lose gambling in Las Vegas this week?"

I sat up almost regretfully. When someone asks me a question like that, I feel obligated to share what I believe.

"I didn't come here to gamble," I said. "I don't do that."

He looked at me quizzically and said, "I've never heard of someone coming to Las Vegas and not gambling. What else is there to do?"

I spent the next two and a half hours describing my work and answering his questions. When we landed in Dallas–Fort Worth, he asked, "Nancy, do you have a brochure about what you do? I'd like to have one."

I pulled one out of my carry-on and handed it to him as I headed toward my connecting flight. Since Mercy Ministries is such an important part of my life, I frequently talk with people about it and many times give them our literature. Once we parted, I didn't give our meeting much thought.

Four weeks later I received a phone call. "Nancy, I don't know if you remember me or not. I'm the man who sat next to you on the flight from Las Vegas."

"Sure I remember. I gave you one of our brochures. Have you been back to Las Vegas?"

"No, I haven't, and that's part of what I'm calling about. Your story prompted so much thought in me during the past few weeks that I haven't been able to get Mercy Ministries off my mind. I had so many things I wanted to tell you that day on the plane, but we ran out of time. I don't think I even told you my name."

He went on: "I became a Christian just three months before I met you. In the past, whenever I was under pressure, I would go to Las Vegas and gamble. This last time it all felt so empty that I decided to go home, but when I got ready to leave, it was like there was almost a physical force holding me there. I couldn't figure it out at the time but finally came to the conclusion that I was supposed to be on that flight to meet you. I'm not used to this 'being led by God' stuff yet, but every time I pray, I keep feeling like there is something I'm supposed to help you build. Are you trying to build something?"

"Yes, actually we already have the land ready to build an unwed mothers' home."

He was silent for a moment, and when he began to speak again, he was crying. "Forty years ago," he told me, "I was born to a teenage girl who had been raped. I never met my birth mother, but I'm sure, considering the circumstances, that if there hadn't been a place for her to go, I would have been aborted.

"I was adopted when I was five days old and have always been very close to my adoptive mother. Last year she died and left me several million dollars. Ever since her death I've been looking for something special I could do in her memory that I thought would be pleasing to her. How much more money do you need?"

I took a deep breath and said, "A hundred and fifty thousand dollars."

"You've got it."

I was absolutely stunned. I couldn't believe what I was hearing. When I regained my composure, I shared with him all the events that had led up to this point. I told him how God had dealt with me to be willing to take in unwed mothers despite the fact that we weren't really equipped to handle their needs. I described how we'd acquired the land and how the need was so great and that we had been praying and believing for God to provide a way to build the home.

When I got off the phone I let out a yell. One of my staff rushed into my office to see if something was wrong.

I was so overjoyed I could hardly speak. "We've got it! We've got it! We've got it!" I was almost dancing around the room.

"Got what?"

"Our new home! The rest of our new home is paid for!"

When the staff realized what I was talking about, we were all literally jumping up and down with joy. The girls had joined us by then and were ecstatic. We phoned all our board members immediately to share the good news and even placed a few calls to some of our supporters to let them know how God had blessed us. We were so excited that we could finally build the home. The man on the plane donated every single penny we still needed to build our first Mercy home for unplanned pregnancies. He secretly visited the home right after we opened its doors because he wanted his gift to be anonymous. He didn't want anyone to know who he was as he walked the halls of the home he had helped build.

God's words still ring in my ears.

"Nancy, you start taking them in and I'll give you the building."

Now we celebrate with hundreds of mothers, adoptive parents, and even grandmothers and grandfathers who watch God follow through on His promises. Just as God provided for our needs in this situation, He has consistently supplied for other needs. Time and time again He has proved Himself to be Jehovah Jireh: "The Lord who provides." God is able to help us not only survive but also achieve success if we serve Him without compromise.

Chapter Eleven

Shelters

"THEREFORE, IF ANYONE is in Christ, he is a new creation; old things have passed away; behold, all things have become new" (2 Cor. 5:17). I have always felt a personal connection to this verse, but if I didn't know better, I'd think God wrote it just for Kaitlen. Her life gives me hope that my life is not about how I started but how I will finish.

The "in Christ" part of the verse means "all in," like in the game of poker. "Going all in" is done by pushing every chip you have to the center of the table—risking *everything* to win. "All in" is what it takes to be made all new in Christ, and it describes Kaitlen perfectly.

What am I holding back from God? Why am I holding on to it? What don't I believe in His Word about His promises? Kaitlen's transformation challenges me with these questions, and her ending excites me because God gave us all a preview of her outcome. But I'll talk about that later.

When I find myself holding on, refusing to open my hand from its tight grip of control, Kaitlen's story whispers, "Go all in, Nancy, go all in!"

And most times, I do.

Watch Kaitlen go all in!

Confused is the best word I know to describe myself as a child growing up. I did not understand what was happening around me or to me. There was so much pain, confusion, and hurt, and most of the time I was in real danger. My house was filled with violence and also serious neglect. Neglect is generally a passive act, but in the case of my family's behavior the neglect was overt and intentional—including the withholding of basic things necessary for survival. I was often not allowed food, water, clothing, or the right to shower or use a toilet. There was abuse in every form. Many people took great pleasure in causing me pain and were intentional and creative in finding ways to hurt or degrade me.

I had very little contact with people outside my house because I was taken out of school after the first grade. While my parents claimed to be homeschooling me, they weren't. My parents caused a lot of problems and drama for the school when they pulled me out, so people avoided us.

I received no further education after I was six years old. This meant complete isolation for me. I was not allowed to develop relationships outside of the house without my parents' supervision. There was no one who might see what was going on with me. I was not protected by anyone, and I was sure that everyone wanted to harm me. What I understood about people was defined by sadism—the deriving of pleasure from cruelty. I learned to view even kindness as a trick—it repeatedly was only a trap to draw me close so someone could more easily hurt me.

I feared people and feared God even more because everything that hurt me was done in His name. My parents were church leaders and used Bible verses to explain why they were doing what they were doing to me. I was told that to resist was to deny God's will, so I did not fight back. I was told God created me for this mistreatment because He loved me and He knew I needed this. I accepted these things as truth, and I believed them. I believed this was part of God's love and character. Everything I heard about God or His love came through this warped filter.

As a small child I used to pray over and over again, "God, please don't let him kill me," while my father would whip me or when others would assault me. I was still very young when my prayer switched to, "God, if You love me at all, You will let me die because I cannot handle this degree of pain. I cannot take this." I learned to numb my emotions and my body. I realized they wanted me to scream and openly show they had caused me pain, so I decided that the only way I could win was to not give them what they wanted. When they would rage and beat me, I did everything I could to hide the pain. Even if they hurt my body, they could not hurt me emotionally, because I no longer had emotions. I stopped feeling everything.

Even though I knew my parents' God to be harsh, I somehow found comfort in Psalm 68:6: "God sets the lonely in families" (NIV). But when I read this verse, I was also confused. What kind of family was this meant to describe? My family was incredibly abusive and dysfunctional. And mine was the only family I was familiar with. Still, this verse spoke deeply to my spirit, and somehow I knew these words were for me—even though there was nothing evident in my daily life to support them.

My childhood aspiration was to sneak off secretly to a homeless shelter the night I turned eighteen, when my parents would no longer be able to control me. But before long it became clear I would not last that long. I started acting out with self-destructive behavior. I was begging for help—for someone, anyone, to notice. The first person I told about my brothers sexually abusing me laughed at me. She thought it was funny that they could be so perverted. The next person I told was a pastor and his wife, who condemned me for being unforgiving and did nothing to help me with the ongoing abuse. The next adult I told was another religious leader who manipulated my vulnerability and became yet another sexual abuser.

Child protective services was involved with my family for as long as I can remember but failed to do anything to really help us. They would show up with police escorts, make threats about taking us away, but never follow through. Because I feared the outside world, I defended my parents for years, telling the lies they instructed me to tell to protect them. But in the desperation of my preteen and early teen years I sent child protective services photographs and reports. They still refused to help. It wasn't until I was fourteen that my brothers and other abusers were investigated. I still remember the shock of the special assault investigator as he shook his head back and forth, saying, "I've been doing this for years, and I have never seen anything like this before."

Finally, as a young teenager, I was taken out of that miserable house. Between ages fourteen and fifteen I was in and out of various foster families and other placements. I was even assigned a bed in a homeless shelter but ended up in a group home. The agencies set up to protect and help me had no idea what to do with me, and with each placement I lost even more of the very tiny piece of hope I had for something more, something real, something that would last. I was also sent back to my parents' house, off and on. My brothers were in jail and my parents' physical abuse was limited because they knew they were being watched, but the trauma they caused was far from over.

Because of my family's violence and desire to control my life and the fact that I was not a ward of the state, my life was in constant danger for years. I didn't know if I would survive. I took it one day at a time, struggling to live just one more day. I was also trying to figure out if I wanted to live at all.

Then I found out about Mercy.

Though I couldn't explain it, I had a deep assurance inside of me that Mercy was my only chance, it was my only hope, and that if I did not go to Mercy, I was going to die. This knowledge was so strong within me that I immediately began the process to get there.

I was fifteen years old when I came to the Mercy home. The last place I'd landed was a state-funded group home, and I was out of options. In fact, after my group home stay I was supposed to go to a homeless shelter, but I got my entrance date to Mercy instead. I arrived at Mercy with very little. Even the clothes I came wearing were donated to me and did not fit me. I also came with no social skills or concept of social expectations. While many broken people can hide behind a smile and appear normal, my issues were very obvious. I had been ignored and unseen by the world for so long that I made no effort to hide my brokenness. I did not know how to hold a conversation with a peer, and could not imagine how to conduct myself in something so simple as sitting down next to someone.

I wore a hooded sweatshirt for the initial months of my stay at Mercy because I wanted to hide my face. I was ashamed to be seen. It had been ingrained in me that I was nothing—not even a human being—and I felt ashamed and guilty if someone looked me in the eyes, thinking they would know what I really was. I also lived in constant fear of assault, and my hood was a comfort because it protected my hair. My father used to pull me off the ground by my hair, and my brothers had set my hair on fire. I always chose a seat in the back row, in an end seat, so I could escape quickly and no one could attack me from behind. I slept under my bed at night because of my fear.

It has been said that it's not paranoia if someone really is out to get you. Because of the trickery and sadism I had experienced, I had learned to analyze every situation I experienced for every possible source of deceit and danger. This fed a powerful fear because I knew what people were capable of. That made it very difficult for me to trust anyone. Even if someone acted in a trustworthy manner, I was convinced it was only to build my trust in order to manipulate and harm me.

I saw God through the same lenses of mistrust and fear. At Mercy I consistently heard about *God* and *love*—two words I was all-too familiar with. It was in the names of God and love that I was sadistically tortured for years. I wanted nothing to do with either, and I had to learn an entirely new definition of love. I didn't believe the promises of Scripture applied to me because I didn't believe I was human. I was resistant to help and love offered to me from God or people, because I did not believe I was worthy of it. Then I discovered the words of Romans 8:38–39, which say that *nothing* in all creation can separate us from the love of God. Even if I wasn't human, even I couldn't separate myself from God's love.

The next step of learning God's character came through the verse in which God says, "I know the plans I have for you . . . plans to prosper you and *not to harm you*" (Jer. 29:11, emphasis added). This verse was God's declaration of His intentions toward me, showing me He was not the sadist I believed He was. I met Jesus at Mercy. The god I had known was far away—he only stooped close to know just how to most deeply hurt you. But through Jesus's gentle love and compassion, I learned who God really is. In Matthew 9:36 I read about Jesus having compassion on people, because when He looked at them, He saw they were harassed and helpless, like sheep without a shepherd. I learned this is how Jesus looks at me, not with malice but with tender love and compassion.

Mercy was a house of healing for me. I think of Isaiah 40:11, where it talks about the Lord gathering His people in His arms and carrying them close to His heart. That describes my time at Mercy. I heard, experienced, and received God's love directly from Him and also through the staff members who chose again and again to love me when I was not very lovable.

At Mercy I learned how to seek God and find God through His Word. Experiencing God through His Word deeply changed my life. I learned to recognize His still, small voice in my spirit. I'd heard His voice before Mercy when He told me He would one day give me a new family and when I felt His leading to come to Mercy. It was wonderful to attach the name "my sweet, gentle Savior" to that voice.

God healed me from the deep grief of my past in ways that were clearly visible. He set me free from shame through Ephesians 5:12–14, which says, "The things done in darkness are things people are ashamed even to speak of. But when they are illuminated, they turn into light" (author paraphrase). God promised me that He would turn the darkness of my past into light, and I knew I no longer needed to be ashamed. I learned the things I used to be ashamed of were now emblems of hope and they would be used to shine into the darkness in the lives of others.

For so long all I wanted was to make it through just one more day, one more minute—to be able to keep living. At Mercy I learned so much more than survival or the denial of heartache. Through the hope, joy, and peace that God grew in me, I learned what it takes to not just survive but thrive. I learned that even though I wasn't legally an adult, every choice I made mattered. Even when I felt my life was out of my control, I still chose how I responded in every circumstance.

I can choose what I believe about myself, choose to value myself, choose to let God heal me, choose to forgive. The choices I made in obedience to Christ and through what I learned at Mercy turned my life from a highway to destruction onto a path of abundant life. I learned that the choices that matter the most are rarely the large glaring ones, but it is the little everyday choices that define me. Learning to submit my thoughts to Christ is probably the primary thing that brought me freedom.

I was a minor when I lived at Mercy, and I had no adult outside of Mercy who wanted good for me or whom I could rely on. The Mercy staff members and my Mercy sisters became my first family. The lessons I received from the girls were often simple, like learning to have fun. Fun? I did not know what this was. I also learned companionship and friendship, and I learned how to let myself be loved in a safe way. I learned how to love people freely and how to be vulnerable. I learned how to spend time with another person in a healthy way.

I remember what a big deal it was for me to watch girls sitting next to each other. I couldn't understand it—how did they do it? Finally, with time and the persistent love of the girls and staff, I learned that even the simplest social interactions are a choice. I had the choice to stop listening to my anxiety telling me the person next to me was going to hurt me. I had to choose to see them as a person, not as a danger. I learned how to value others and love them, seeing past my own self and my own fears.

Because I received no financial support from my biological parents or others outside Mercy, I was unable to purchase things I needed. I received a lot of practical assistance while at Mercy, such as staff donating cash to pay for my needs like shampoo. When I lost my luggage on my way back from Christmas break with a foster family, losing all the clothes and gifts Mercy and others had given me, Mercy gave me clothing to replace all I had lost. The love of the staff and the provision Mercy made possible were truly remarkable and a demonstration of God's goodness to me.

I graduated Mercy when I was sixteen years old, and God worked through Mercy to prepare the way for my next placement. Mercy found a place for me at a residential Bible school and even provided a scholarship for me to attend. While attending this school, I knew I needed to not only continue my Bible studies but also further my regular education. Even though the Mercy education director had tried to work with me while I was there, I was simply too far behind to catch up. Thankfully, after Mercy, I was able to get my GED. But I still had a long way to go to catch up to the true college entrance expectations. Certainly at the time of earning my GED no one suspected how much academia would influence my life.

My life after Mercy has not always been easy, but it has been a very beautiful and incredible experience. No matter what happens, no matter what I face, I am sometimes amazed just to think, "I am alive! I am twenty-five years old and I am alive!" I wasn't supposed to live to be eighteen, and I now live a vibrant, full life.

Not only am I still alive, but also God has given me so much more. Through the relationships I developed at Mercy, God gave me a family. Nancy also spoke Psalm 68:6 over me at my graduation, saying God had given her this verse for me. God was not done restoring my family yet! Shortly before my eighteenth birthday, I met a couple in their midforties with no children. This couple became my family, giving me their name and a place in their home. I lived with them for almost three years, by far the longest time I have lived anywhere in more than ten years. God gave me more than I could have asked or imagined.

God brought a tremendous amount of healing through my adopted family. I struggled with a lot of fear at first, but I learned to love them and to allow them to love me. While I was at Mercy, God planted in me the seeds of forgiveness for those who had hurt me. He used my adoptive parents' healing love as the catalyst to deepen those seeds of forgiveness. At Mercy I had begun to pray every day that God would help me to forgive. I learned to walk in forgiveness, and I learned to choose to forgive.

After years of learning forgiveness, God began to show me how He also loves the people who hurt me. My heart began to ache for their brokenness. God gave me a true love for them. I have no contact with them, but I hope and pray God brings them the healing He has given me.

After receiving my GED, I began college with the dream of working in medicine. Once I recognized that fear was the only thing standing between me and my education, I decided to defy fear and go as far as I could. I enrolled in college as a premedical student, on the path to becoming a physician. I worked very hard to catch up academically, studying ten or more hours each day. I had to learn basic concepts like how to add fractions. The Lord has blessed me and given me so much favor and grace to not only catch up but also to exceed every expectation. I graduated from college at age twenty-two with a bachelor of science degree in biology and a bachelor of arts in German language and literature—*summa cum laude*.

Shortly before my graduation I was awarded a US Fulbright scholarship. I received a ten-month grant to go to Germany, where

I conducted medical and epidemiological research at a German university hospital. I worked primarily with coma patients and analyzed factors that impacted their functional and behavioral outcome. After my Fulbright term in Munich, I was awarded an extended period of research through a further Fulbright Grantee period, a "Fulbright Internship." I was one of a few selected out of all the research Fulbrighters in Germany. In total I spent sixteen months as a US Fulbrighter, representing my country as an ambassador. After my internship I was employed by the university where I conducted my research. I lived in Germany a total of one and a half years.

While living in Germany, I was accepted to a master's program in epidemiology and intended to stay in Germany longer—but God had other plans. In the years before I left for Germany, an important friendship was slowly developing with Nathan, a man whom I met during my undergraduate work. We were becoming close during my last months in America, and Nathan told me he felt as if he was losing his best friend with my move. During my initial months of adjustments and culture shock in Germany, I reached out often to Nathan as a connection back to the United States, and our friendship became much deeper. After I had been in Germany for six months, we realized that God had more for our relationship than just friendship. We dated through Skype and phone calls, with rare visits. This long-distance relationship sharpened our communication skills, for which we are forever grateful. Though it was difficult to be apart, God was drawing us together even over the distance, and our relationship grew rapidly. In the spring of 2012 I moved home to America, and we got married in my adoptive parents' backyard.

I am so grateful to God for again expanding the beautiful family He has given me and for the sweet, fun, and healing relationship I have with my husband. It is only by a miracle of God that I am able to be married. I, who feared men and never wanted to be married, now love and delight in my husband and my marriage! God's gift of my husband has given me the sweetest part of my life that I could ever imagine.

My husband and I live in the United States, where I am working as a private tutor, sharing my love for education with others and preventing them from having academic deficiencies such as the ones I faced. I also mentor young women and meet with foster children. It is my greatest honor that the Lord allows my life to touch others. I have recently been accepted to medical school and am looking forward to how God will further my ability to reach others as a physician. I want to be a competent and compassionate physician, but I also want to teach, passing on medical knowledge to the next generation of doctors. I am so grateful for the beautiful work God did in me at Mercy Ministries, and I am confident that He will keep His promise to complete it (Phil. 1:6).

God completely changed my life—my mind, my spirit, my body, and my heart—at Mercy Ministries. Through my time there, God gave me my first chance at life.

My first memory of Kaitlen was seeing her sitting in a classroom at Mercy listening to a guest speaker. I'd heard about a fifteen-year-old coming in who was extremely broken, but I had not yet met her.

I saw a girl in the back row wearing a hooded sweatshirt that covered her entire face. Her head was down, and it didn't take me long to figure out that it was Kaitlen. None of us working with Kaitlen saw much of her face for the first few months. After we all read her file, we knew why she was adamant about hiding in that hooded sweatshirt. We'd never had a girl who was a first grade dropout. We'd never faced the challenge of working with a girl who could not read or write.

About two months in I met with our program director and our director of education. They agreed it would be impossible to work with Kaitlen using our conventional methods, given her limitations. We made adjustments and focused on her spiritual life and bringing healing to all the damage from her past. We prayed with her and talked with her about a personal relationship with Christ. We prayed for wholeness and health to come to Kaitlen.

Because she had no family, we were also committed to helping with her education *after* Mercy. At the very least our goal was for her to attain her GED.

The next week my dear friends Pastors Tom and Jane Hamon from Santa Rosa Beach, Florida, were scheduled to be our guest speakers. Not only do they pastor a church but also they have a very strong and powerful prophetic gift. I usually ask them to speak at each Mercy home at least one time each year. They pray for all the girls individually and encourage them, speaking God's heart to each girl. Whenever Pastors Tom and Jane come, we record their prophetic words so our residents can listen to them and be encouraged during tough times. The apostle Paul spoke to Timothy about this: "Take the prophetic words you receive and wage warfare with them" (1 Tim. 1:18, author paraphrase).

As Jane stood behind the podium that morning in 2003, Kaitlen was still trapped inside her hooded sweatshirt. She sat in the middle row of our classroom shrouded in fear and shame.

After Jane finished speaking, she walked down the aisle and straight up to Kaitlen. Jane took her by the hand and asked if she could pray for her. Kaitlen initially hesitated but then shook her head yes.

Let me share with you a portion of her prophetic word for Kaitlen:

> The Lord says, "My daughter, I've given you a brilliant mind. I've given you a huge capacity to learn. I've given you such an ability to learn that I'm going to open up the doors of education to you. You're going to go to college and you're even going to go on full scholarship and you're going to have multiple degrees, and what I do through you is even going to be so amazing that high school principals will call and say, 'Would you please come and share your story to our students?'"

As much as I respect my friends and know the accuracy of their gifting, this day I was skeptical and doubted their word for

Kaitlen. How could someone who was a first grade dropout end up with multiple degrees and opportunities for scholarships?

I felt like hiding. I slouched down in my seat and thought, "Oh well, I guess everyone misses the mark occasionally." Yet as you have read, I was wrong. God's word for Kaitlen did come to pass. How thankful I am for people like Pastors Jane and Tom who have the faith to trust God to use them in this way!

That day proved to be a turning point in Kaitlen's life and mine. A true prophetic gift can be powerful, especially in the life of someone as broken as Kaitlen. And even though I doubted, God was faithful to His word, and my faith grew as His truths were revealed in Kaitlen's life. I've heard Pastors Jane and Tom speak over hundreds of people since 2003 and have had the honor of watching God fulfill His promises through these dear friends. I have never again doubted them or my God who promises to speak to those who will listen.

CHAPTER TWELVE

The Why
Behind the What

OVER THE YEARS I have listened to the experiences of thousands of broken young women. Many of them sought help from local churches before they ever walked through the doors at Mercy. Some of them had responded to altar calls and received Christ as their Savior and yet still did not feel accepted by the congregations. They felt a sense of rejection. They had messed-up backgrounds and their minds had not yet been renewed by God's Word. They were not discipled, and they struggled to accept themselves. They felt judged and rejected, so they left their churches without ever getting connected.

That breaks my heart. Jesus was disgusted with hypocritical rule keepers who were quick to judge others. He said, "These people draw near to Me with their mouth, and honor Me with their lips, but their heart is far from Me" (Matt. 15:8). Throughout the New Testament Jesus was constantly challenging the scribes and Pharisees about their self-righteousness and their unwillingness to show love and mercy. In turn they criticized Him for hanging out with sinners and rule breakers. His response was that "it is not the healthy who need a doctor, but the sick. But go and learn what this means: 'I desire mercy, not sacrifice.' For I have not come to call the righteous, but sinners" (Matt. 9:12–13, NIV). And James 2:13 reminds us that "mercy triumphs over judgment."

We all need to take these scriptures to heart. We *must* have compassion for people we don't understand. We have not walked the paths they have walked. When people come to church who look different from us, we shouldn't judge them. And it is not just a matter of smiling and being careful with our words. Sometimes we may even give ourselves brownie points for not being like them. This pretentiousness is what the Pharisees were so good at.

We must remember that when judgment is present, compassion is absent. Sadly, visitors who do not make our "cut" are labeled *outsiders,* and leave with even more baggage than when they arrived. Instead of offering fresh hope, we load them down with greater hopelessness. I'm reminded of a young girl who came to Mercy in the late eighties with an unplanned pregnancy. Her church kicked her out for being pregnant and would not allow her to come back. The very place where she should have received unconditional love and support was the place that turned her away. This makes no sense. It is the same thing as a hospital turning away someone in need of medical care. One of the main purposes of the church is to care for the wounded—at least the church as God intended.

What are we thinking? No wonder Jesus warned us against judging others.

> Judge not, that you be not judged. For with what judgment you judge, you will be judged; and with the measure you use, it will be measured back to you. And why do you look at the speck in your brother's eye, but do not consider the plank in your own eye? Or how can you say to your brother, "Let me remove the speck from your eye"; and look, a plank is in your own eye? Hypocrite! First remove the plank from your own eye, and then you will see clearly to remove the speck from your brother's eye.
> —Matthew 7:1–5

The real issue in this passage involves dealing with the sin in our own lives. In order for us to see clearly from God's perspective, we must first remove the "plank" of self-righteousness from our lives.

Judgment clouds our vision and keeps us from helping others the way they need to be helped. Our judgment blocks our view of the situation. Other people are not our standard. The standard is God's Word and Jesus Christ. Really, this whole book is about taking the planks (obstructions) out of our own eyes so that we can see clearly the *why* behind the *what* and bring healing to the brokenhearted.

God wants us to get involved, but first we have to deal with ourselves. If we are going to love others, we have to see them through God's eyes. If we ask Him, He will give us eyes to see the way He sees people and a heart to love them the way He loves them.

We are supposed to react the same way Jesus did when He encountered people who had sinned.

This brings to mind again the story of the woman who was caught in the act of adultery. The scribes and Pharisees brought her to Jesus, asking Him what He thought should be done with her. They weren't so interested in the woman but were more focused on finding something with which they could accuse Jesus. They were extremely jealous of Him and the great crowds that were drawn to Him. Jesus extended compassion, love, and mercy as never before seen. Who on earth wouldn't draw close to His love? John 8:7 tells us that when they continued asking Him that same question of what to do with the woman, Jesus raised up from writing in the dirt and said, "He who is without sin among you, let him throw a stone at her first." That did it. Those words were so powerful and convicting that one by one they dropped the rocks and went their own ways.

The woman stood alone with Jesus. He told her He was not there to condemn or accuse her, but that He had a much better life in store for her, better than the life she was living. Jesus said, "I am the light of the world. He who follows Me shall not walk in darkness, but have the light of life" (v. 12). The cool thing about Jesus here is that He doesn't just say, "Don't sin anymore." He tells us how not to!

If we are to represent Christ well in this world, then we have to learn to love people unconditionally, even when they have sinned greatly. Regardless of what the sin is, our job is to keep ourselves in the love of God, releasing God's mercy and compassion to people who need it (Jude 20–23).

We would do well to have the same mind-set about others that God has about us, captured for us in these beautiful, compassionate words:

> He has not dealt with us according to our sins, nor punished us according to our iniquities. For as the heavens are high above the earth, *so* great is His mercy toward those who fear Him; as far as the east is from the west, *so* far has He removed our transgressions from us.
> —PSALM 103:10–12, EMPHASIS ADDED

This is good news for all of us. If we want to receive mercy, then we have to be willing to extend mercy to others, regardless of what they have done. This is what it means to be a Christian...a true follower of Christ.

Once our hearts are in the right place, there's no limit to what God can do with us. I recently visited our St. Louis home and spoke with one of our residents who told me that before coming to Mercy she had been in *thirty-eight* different treatment programs. She had only been at Mercy for three weeks, but told me this was the first time she ever had hope that she could actually break free from her addiction. As the realization hit me of how much money this young woman had spent on treatment programs over the years, my mind went immediately to Mark 5:25–34, the story about a woman who had experienced something very similar.

"Now a certain woman had a flow of blood for twelve years, and had suffered many things from many physicians. She had spent all that she had and was no better, but rather grew worse" (vv. 25–26).

Just like so many of our girls, this woman spent everything she had on doctors who tried to treat the symptoms, and instead of getting better, she just got worse. She was out of money. She was out of options. But when Jesus touches someone, He goes straight to the heart, right to the very root of the problem. The Jesus factor changed the rules she lived under. Jesus set her free. That is what sets Mercy apart from other programs, because apart from Him we can do nothing (John 15:5). We are so aware that it is not Mercy Ministries or any of our staff that bring healing, but rather the Great Physician Himself, the only One who can bring *real* transformation.

That's the testimony given by so many of the girls who walk through the doors of Mercy Ministries. Hundreds of thousands of dollars spent on treatment programs. Many options tried with no success. I know that there are many wonderful people who work in treatment programs and who do care about their patients. But I also know from my time in the government system that caring workers—and even Christ followers—are often limited by the systems they work under. I cared deeply for the girls under my watch at the juvenile detention facility and wanted to help them, but the system wouldn't allow me to tell the truth about the One who could transform their lives.

That's why treatment facilities have their limitations. If we don't believe in Jesus's words, "It is finished," we will try to keep "finishing it" by our own strength. We will keep trying to transform our lives on our own, and we will fail. I believe this is why treatment programs often ultimately don't work—because they are about changing lives through behavior modification and coping mechanisms. But Christ comes in and gives us a *new* heart and a *new* spirit.

Our girls' transformations begin with the freedom and forgiveness of a relationship with Jesus Christ—one that's available to all of us. When Jesus died on the cross, He descended into hell and demanded that Satan give Him the keys to death and the grave. Jesus never sinned (see Hebrews 4:15), so hell had no legal right to keep Him there. Satan couldn't hold Him there because it is a place of separation from God. Jesus paid the price of sin and death for everyone who has ever been born. And then He rose again and appeared to the disciples, saying, "Go and tell everyone what I have done for them" (Mark 16:14–15, author's paraphrase).

Jesus commands us to embrace the new covenant of His salvation and love—including that no one is beyond His reach and that He paid the price for all. Our job is to tell people they don't have to stay in captivity, the price has been paid, and they just have to receive it. We tell the girls who come to Mercy:

> Now that you've confessed your sins and received Christ, it's time for a paradigm shift in your mind. You're not fighting *for* freedom—you're fighting from a place of victory. Jesus already paid the price and defeated your past and your sin, so now you need to believe that *it is finished* and fight from that place.
>
> "There is therefore now no condemnation to those who are in Christ Jesus, who do not walk according to the flesh, but according to the Spirit" (Rom. 8:1).
>
> "Present your bodies a living sacrifice, holy, acceptable to God, which is your reasonable service" (Rom. 12:1).
>
> Now live a new life. Learn who you are in Christ. Your body is now a temple of the Holy Spirit. It's not to be cut on, abused with drugs, or abused with food. Your body is now a place where Christ lives. Dedicate your body to God as a living sacrifice. His sacrifice was that He took our place on the cross so that we can be free. If He died to set us free, is it too much to ask that we live for Him and dedicate our bodies to Him?

No, it is not too much to ask. We give all of who we are and all of who we are not to the One who makes all things new in Christ Jesus. We love fiercely and forgive freely, knowing that we have been given much more than we can ever give back. And in my heart that is *why* God is *what* He is to me...love and freedom.

Appendix

More to the Story...

I N THIS APPENDIX you will read more inspiring stories of young women who have walked through the doors of one of our Mercy Ministries homes. Some of them had been scarred by years of abuse. Some of them had chosen a path of rebellion that led them into a darkness they suddenly found themselves unable to escape. Some of them had led good lives but made a few mistakes that had devastating consequences.

All of them sought after God to help them, and they chose

to come to Mercy Ministries to find the healing they needed and desired. All of them found their lives undeniably changed by the power of God. All of them came to understand that nothing is too hard for God.

When I was younger, my heroes were sports stars—the player who caught the winning touchdown pass or who sunk the winning basket. I truly thought these incredible athletes were the real heroes—until I met the courageous girls who come to Mercy. Despite feeling great pain, they come to Mercy and bravely surrender their lives to God.

I believe that when you read the heart-gripping stories of these girls, my heroes, you'll see how a heart of compassion can make a huge difference in the life of another. Let their stories, in their own words, raw and real, show you that there is always a why behind the what.

CALLI

Before coming to Mercy Ministries at the age of twenty, I was extremely angry at myself, my family, the world, and God. I grew up hearing the truth about Jesus's death on the cross, but I questioned whether God really existed. I struggled with the question tons of people wrestle with: If God exists, why do bad things happen to good people? I partially hoped God didn't exist because I had so much anger toward Him for creating a world with so much pain, suffering, and injustice. I grew up in a good family and had loving parents who taught me good morals and made me feel loved, but there were things that happened in my childhood that they didn't know until a decade after the fact.

I was the youngest of four kids and had an identical twin sister who was my best friend and biggest competitor. My parents divorced when I was six but maintained a friendship where they shared custody of us four kids. My mom began dating another man who became abusive to her, which sent her into a bout of clinical depression. When I was seven, her boyfriend began sexually abusing me on a fairly regularly basis. After the first time I tried to tell my twin sister and older brother about the abuse to make sure it wasn't happening to them too, but after telling them, they didn't take action like I thought they might. I didn't go into details of what I had experienced because of embarrassment, so they never grasped the severity of what had happened. I took their response as rejection. I was crushed by their rejection and grew angry with everyone. I thought that if my own siblings wouldn't believe me, no one would.

The sexual abuse continued for three years. My abuser had silenced me with fear, guilt, and shame. He convinced me that if I told anyone, they wouldn't believe me, or that they'd be hurt if they did believe me, especially my mom. I believed him at the time because I had witnessed him physically and verbally abusing my mom. Being abused forced me to grow up quickly and stole my ability to trust people. I built walls around my heart and became a tomboy because I feared being weak, vulnerable, or used for someone else's pleasure like my abuser had done.

After three years of the abuse I reached out for help again and told my best friend at school about it. Three days later my best friend died in a freak accident—he was electrocuted while draining the bathtub and blow-drying his hair. After being brainwashed for a few years, I thought I was to blame for his death because my abuser had warned me that anyone I told would reject it or be hurt if they did believe me. My best friend had believed me and now he was dead. Although it's illogical thinking, I was only nine at the time and refused to talk to an adult about my best friend's death. Shortly after this we moved away with my mom so she could get out of the abusive relationship. After this incident I believed the lie that anyone I got close to would get hurt and it was my fault because I was a horrible, evil person.

I stayed silent about the abuse and grew up as a tomboy, always acting tough, rarely smiling, and never letting my family hug me. I always wanted to be alone and trusted no one. Sometimes my family would joke innocently that I was the evil twin since I was usually rude to them, and this just reinforced the lie that I was a bad person. My family knew something was wrong but had no clue what had happened to cause me to be so unfriendly and unhappy. It was difficult being a twin during this time because everyone always compared us to each other, and I always felt inferior since I was not as friendly or well liked.

My mom remarried when I was thirteen, and we moved to Omaha, which was the big city compared to small-town Nebraska. I fell further into depression, self-hatred, and anger toward my family. My mom tried to get me to see a counselor a few times, but I refused. I agreed to go on antidepressants to satisfy my mom's concern but refused to talk about any of the root issues. I had no hope for being free from self-hatred and the desire to die. I thought death was the only way I would be at peace and became obsessed with thinking about it.

I started cutting and hitting myself, doing dangerous stunts and anything to feel alive because I felt numb from all the internal pain. The only way I knew I was alive was if I felt pain or saw blood. I began visiting some pro-self-harm and pro-suicide websites and chat rooms. I began talking with other people who felt the same way I did, and it was the only place I didn't feel so alone. My goal in life from age thirteen became to die physically since I believed I was already emotionally and spiritually dead. I didn't know if God existed at this point, and if He did, I hated Him because I didn't understand why He allowed me to go through so much or why He didn't protect me like He promised to in His Word.

I was an A student and good athlete and tried to find my identity in these things. I started dating when I was fourteen, messing around with boys, stealing beer and cigarettes from my stepdad to use by myself to numb the pain. All through high school I put on the front that I was fine and was even voted best sense of humor in my graduating class, but I suffered silently every day to stay alive. I frequently went on the pro-suicide chat rooms just to have someone to talk to where I could be real rather than wear a mask that I was fine. I used alcohol, smoking, prescription meds, cutting, exercising, boys, and sports to cope. My senior year of high school I was raped at a college frat party

I attended and lost my virginity. This incident made me grow colder and harder than I already was.

I went to college at University of Nebraska at Lincoln because that's what my parents wanted, and I didn't plan on living past twenty-one. I partied hard the first several months and joined the rugby team, hoping I'd get seriously injured. There were two girls on the team who were total Jesus freaks and saw through all the anger and tough girl attitude. I treated them horribly because they represented a God I couldn't understand. The ruder I was to them, the more they went out of their way to love me, and eventually one of them explained the love of Jesus and His desire for my well-being in a way I'd never heard. I had formulated a suicide plan and written notes to all my family members and friends a couple nights before, but hearing about God's love gave me a glimmer of hope that God was real. I gave my life to Jesus in the back of an old coffee shop and decided that since I had tried everything the world has to offer for happiness, I might as well try God before giving up completely.

I quit drinking, smoking, cutting, dating, popping pills, cussing, and everything else I thought was unholy. I tried to commit my life fully to the Lord at age eighteen and went from a life of unrighteousness to self-righteousness. I didn't know how to receive God's mercy, grace, and forgiveness for my sins, so I tried to fix myself. But the depression and suicidal thoughts wouldn't leave and only got worse when I didn't have any of my old coping mechanisms. I didn't dare tell my new Christian friends how much I was struggling with suicide because I thought now that I was a Christian I couldn't have those problems or thoughts.

I had to take an autobiography writing class in school and write about my childhood for the big class project, and it brought everything I was struggling with out into the light. I couldn't wear a mask and act like everything was OK anymore. The abuse, anger, hurt, guilt, and shame I'd never dealt with couldn't hide anymore, and after a year of struggling to live holy on my own strength, I knew I needed serious help.

As the depression increased after opening up about my past through writing, I fell back into cutting, drinking, smoking, and using prescription drugs to deal with the inner turmoil. I only felt more guilty, ashamed, and hopeless when they didn't work. I ended up telling my parents about the childhood abuse and how much I was really struggling with depression and suicide because I knew I needed help or I wasn't going to survive. I was eventually hospitalized for suicide and severe depression after months of counseling and antidepressants didn't work. Doctors couldn't figure out what to do with me since no combination of medication, therapy, or counseling helped; they only convinced me more that I was never going to be free from depression and all the tormenting thoughts until I was dead. Doctors used electroconvulsive therapy (shock treatment) as a last resort because I was so suicidal. I had a series of twenty shock treatments within two months and had severe short-term memory loss as a side effect. The treatment worked in that it took the edge off of my ambition to die, but it also created a new set of issues to deal with. I began hallucinating and struggled to decipher what was real and not real.

I had stumbled upon Mercy Ministries' website months before I was hospitalized and read several of the girls' testimonies while searching for a pro-suicide chat room that changed its web address. Doctors wanted to put me in the state psych ward indefinitely since they didn't know how else to help me, but I applied to Mercy Ministries as a last hope. I applied because my family wouldn't give up on me, and it hurt me to see how much I was hurting them by wanting to die.

I went to Mercy Ministries in St. Louis in July 2007 and was there for more than seven months. I was very resistant to the staff and the program when I went because I had been promised by so many doctors and therapists that their treatment would help me, and they only left me more wounded; so I had a lot of walls up coming into the home. It took several months until I finally let the walls down and let God back into my life. The way the staff continued to love me when I was so rude, harsh, and hard-hearted amazed me. They showed me that the love of Christ is unconditional, and they helped me learn how to trust again. While there I learned the truth about God, Satan, and myself. I realized several of the lies I had grown up believing about myself and was healed and set free from all the guilt, shame, addictions, and death wishes. God broke down the walls I had built around my heart and restored my mind, spirit, and soul to health. I learned how to fight against the enemy, pray, study the Word, and how to trust in the Lord. After graduating the program in February 2008 I moved back home to Omaha to restore relationships with my family.

God has done amazing things in my life since graduating from Mercy over five years ago, and I'm excited to see the full plans He has for my life come to fruition. I know that my life is more about God and His plans than it is about me. I still have a huge passion for justice, and I trust that God will give me an outlet for this passion He's put in me. I'm convinced that God is good in every season of life, rain or shine, and I have no fear of death because I know where I'm going. I graduated with my bachelor's degree in criminology and criminal justice in May 2011 and am currently working on my master's right now with a full scholarship. I plan on getting my PhD so I can teach at the college level and do quality research to impact America's criminal justice system and a lot of the flaws within it (as long as God continues funding me through the program I'm in where I'm actually getting paid to go to school—how cool is that!). God has turned my ashes into beauty and given me joy for mourning (Isa. 61:3).

HOLLY

Before attending Mercy Ministries, I had struggled for five years with an eating disorder. But for an even longer time, probably starting in my early childhood, I had always hated myself. I hated the way that I looked. I hated my personality and the fact that I was so quiet and shy. I hated that my family was poor and that other kids judged me for not having the things that they had. I hated that my parents were not able to attend many of my track meets or basketball games. And I felt that they did not take time to spend to get to know me because they were too focused on work or fighting with each other. I felt like a wallflower, invisible, and that no one noticed me. We moved often, and I went to five different schools growing up. I was the new kid one too many times, and lunchtime without friends was the most miserable experience.

Eventually the control of food became a friend to me. Food made me feel comforted when no one else would. It didn't seem like a big deal at first. A few times a week when I was feeling stressed or lonely, I would binge and purge. Meaning I would eat food and then throw it up so that I wouldn't gain weight from it. I would do whatever it took to get food—steal food, steal money, or get food from the trash can. Or I would not eat for a couple of days if I started to feel like I was gaining weight. I remember telling people that I was fasting or that I had already eaten if my friends were going out to eat and I didn't want to join them.

However, it didn't take long before this occasional action began to master my life. It dictated my every thought. I kept trying to quit, but I couldn't stop no matter how hard I tried. I didn't know how to be free. I figured that if this was how my life was going to look, I didn't want to live it anymore. It was worse because I was a Christian, and I was doing exactly what I should not have been doing. On the outside I'm sure I seemed to have things together; I played sports, served in Christian ministry leadership roles, attended youth group, volunteered in the community, and made perfect grades. I even got into nursing school in college somehow. However, I hated myself so much for living this double life. The only way out was to not be here anymore. I prayed that God would just take my life.

One night after I had purged my food, my nose started bleeding really hard. But it didn't stop, and I didn't stop it. I hoped that this would be my last night if I could just keep bleeding. I remember looking around. Blood was everywhere. This was one of the darkest moments in my life. But for some reason God had different plans for me. He did not want that to be the end. I'm not sure what happened, but the bleeding stopped. Occurrences such as this happened a few more times. I continued to just survive day after day without any hope for my future and becoming emotionally avoidant to anything that required feeling in my life. I dropped out of almost all of my classes my junior year of nursing school.

A few months later I heard about Mercy Ministries from my church in Nashville, Tennessee. I applied to the program at Mercy and could not wait to arrive at the home. Mercy Ministries represented the opportunity and hope to start a new life where I actually wanted to live. I went into Mercy with my head low, embarrassed about getting myself to a point in life that I could not get out of by myself. But I was so thankful that I had somewhere to help me with the mess I had gotten myself into, and I was thankful that people wanted to help me change.

Mercy Ministries changed my life. I would not be where I am today without having gone through the six-month program at Mercy. They taught me to trust God again. Before, I hated

Him for letting bad things happen in my life. I hated Him for not being there for me. I learned that He had never left me since I accepted Him into my heart as a five-year-old little girl. Instead, He had been with me ever since, and the things that broke my heart broke His heart worse.

I did not understand why God would care so much for me, a sinner who had destroyed her life. But He offered me forgiveness and love when I least deserved it. God mostly showed me these things through the staff at Mercy and through the teachings and readings that we learned from.

The staff really cared about me. I remember having so many talks and prayers with the staff. They were always ready to listen and offer me a biblical perspective for my questions. They made me feel loved, heard, and like a beloved child of God. I am so grateful to the Mercy staff...I will never be the same.

Although I am originally from Nashville, Tennessee, St. Louis has been my home for more than four years now. I could never have pictured my life without an eating disorder and depression. I have not participated in bingeing or purging or skipping meals since the day that I arrived at Mercy. Thank God! My mentors, friends, and church have significantly impacted my life after Mercy. I now hold a bachelor's in psychology from a university in St. Louis. I have had the opportunity to work with middle and high school students at ZOE Ministries and to travel on mission trips to Costa Rica with the youth to help spread the gospel. It has been such a privilege to work with young girls. Many of them are going through struggles, whether it is an eating disorder, self-harm, depression, or insecurity. I also traveled to Belize on a medical missions trip. I am currently working toward my BSN with hopes to become a pediatric nurse and continue to serve God in many ways!

JEN

I have always known God. My earliest memories are flooded with the knowledge of His presence. I can remember having tea parties with Jesus in the woods near my house or dancing around the statues of Him at the nearby Catholic church. I would sit on His bronze lap and imagine Him speaking directly to me, like any Father would. The greatest mystery in my relationship with God will always be where it originated; my family never really went to church, and I don't remember my parents ever talking about God. I am convinced that these foundational encounters with Jesus provided me with the grace to face what would become the most confusing time in my life.

My dad and I were very close. I was an abnormally active child, and he never seemed to run out of energy or patience. I didn't care that he drank too much and always fought with my mom. When he was drunk, he was carefree and fun. I didn't understand what was happening when my mom sat me down to explain that everything would stay the same and that I didn't have to worry. I would still see my dad on the weekends and could call him whenever I wanted. I didn't know that my parents' separation would change the rest of my life and completely restructure the way I felt about men. Nothing stayed the same.

My sixth birthday marked the entrance into my first catechism classes. I passed the exams with ease and quickly advanced through the stages that would earn me my first Holy Communion. I dreamed one day I would become a nun or a missionary, or both, like Mother Teresa. My catechism instructor told me that I could never be a nun because nuns don't shoot rubber bands in class or lock their instructors out of the classroom. Despite my instructor I continued to advance in class, sometimes memorizing chapters of Old Testament scripture for extra credit. I also began playing as many sports as I could, desperate to recapture my father's waning attention. If I wasn't at church or school, I was in the yard practicing my batting or on the street shooting free throws.

My best friend's older brother began to sexually abuse me just before my ninth birthday. He told me how mature I was compared to his sisters and how beautiful I was for my age. It felt nice to have male affirmation once again, since I hardly saw my father by this point. He would invite me over to help me with my basketball drills, but we always wound up locked in his room. My mom began to ask him to babysit during the nights that she had to work late.

In the beginning he would bargain with me, giving me rewards for complying. After I got up enough courage to say no, the threats began. After he got me drunk, he would undress me and lay on top of me. He made me watch pornography while he lay on top of my naked body. When he tried to enter me, I punched his face. He punched me back in the stomach, and I lost my breath. He told me that if I ever said no to him again, he would kill me, and I believed him. After that, I did everything he asked; every encounter was more degrading than the last. I finally got up the courage to scream, but he covered my mouth so fast, no one heard. He used a knife to threaten me and would press it against my throat as he performed acts on me. I remember disconnecting when I was little. I would shut off all of my body's responses. My vision would get blurry, and I became numb. The vodka helped, and sometimes I would even take my mom's painkillers before I went to his house. Whenever he started to touch me, I tried to imagine being in another place, but whenever he spoke or made noise, I would be thrust back into reality and all of my senses were engaged as he used me. Most times I would wake up on the couch or in bed. He would use me and then put me back where I belonged. When I woke up, there were usually signs of what happened the night before. My bottom would throb with pain; I would be sore between my legs and swollen. Sometimes there were scratch marks and bruises. During this time I began to self-harm by hitting my hands and fingers with a hammer, running my bike into cement walls, or stabbing and piercing myself with sewing needles. I didn't know why I did this; I thought it was because I was bored or because I thought blood was cool, but now I see the connection because I only acted on these behaviors when I felt overwhelmed or disconnected. The violent abuse continued for three years, and I stopped trying to be perfect. The abuse made me feel so out of control, so I acted out in school, determined that no one else would have power over me. I started smoking when I was nine and began to hang out with a dangerous group of kids. I sold prescription pills at school, some supplied through my "friends" and some from my mom's stash. I earned my reputation by picking locks and breaking into cars, houses, and classrooms. I would do anything to be accepted. If I didn't feel like being in school, I would purge to make my teachers think I was sick so I could go home. I kept this trick in my arsenal, but its function changed dramatically in high school.

I eventually left the Catholic Church after the priest harshly scolded me for ringing the bells at the wrong time during mass. I began attending a Baptist church with a neighbor and instantly felt at home. I became actively involved with the youth program and spent the summer before my freshman year at Bible camp. I came back from camp on fire for God and excited to begin my first year of Christian high school.

My freshman year launched the roller coaster that would take me through the ups and downs of my high school career. I had trouble adjusting to a completely new school system and the authority that went with it. I quickly discovered that my rebellion would not be tolerated. After my first trip to the head-master's office my passion for the new school year and for God left as quickly as it had come. I decided that if I couldn't be perfect, I would be the exact opposite. I opposed all the rules and enjoyed finding loopholes in the rule book, frustrating my teachers to no end. After school I would sneak out to parties with my new friends. Although I never drank, I enjoyed the chaos of the party scene; it was another thing that made me feel in control.

That summer I began attending the nondenominational

church associated with my school. My group of friends began to change as I became more involved. I'm convinced that their support along with God's providence brought me through the years to come. My sophomore year exemplified a brand-new Jen: I excelled in school and was voted class president. I played four varsity sports and really enjoyed being involved with youth group.

That summer I went on a missions trip with a friend from school. We spent two weeks in Brazil. During this trip I was blessed to be able to see God's hand perform miracles and break down walls that had been constructed for years. I was asked to preach to more than two thousand Brazilians. That trip changed the course of my life and built up my faith in ways I could never explain. It also prepared me for the challenges ahead.

My senior year was hectic; I had slowly begun to feel the weight of all the activities I had committed to. The self-harm continued, especially cutting and purging. I ran cross-country, and it seemed like no matter how many hours of practice I put in, I could never be good enough. I thought if I were skinnier, I would be a better athlete. I restricted food and purged daily— yet another secret I had to keep.

My relationship with my mom got worse and worse. I couldn't even go home many nights because I knew there would inevitably be something we'd end up fighting about. I embraced my new life as a vagabond and didn't even mind sleeping in my car or on a beach near the school. It was adventurous and new, but mostly it was safe because I was in control. I didn't let anyone know about my situation because I had too much pride. My mom eventually kicked me out one night in a rage, and I left with a backpack full of food, my school uniform, and my soccer cleats. My youth pastor was incredibly supportive, but I could never be fully open with her about all of my struggles.

I continued to go to school, washing my uniforms in the locker room showers and sleeping under the stars when I had nowhere to stay. Even though this was one of the most trying times in my life, I wouldn't trade it for the world. I had to learn to depend on God for the simplest of necessities, which cultivated a trust beyond explanation. My passion was real, but I neglected myself and pushed the years of silent abuse to the back burner. I just wanted to forget about it.

By the middle of the year my lethargy turned to exhaustion and my grades slipped dramatically. God saw my fatigue, and by some miracle a man at my church heard about my situation and offered to let me live on one of his properties for the rest of the year.

I moved into my little house, and by the sheer grace of God and consistent support from my youth pastor, I graduated high school. That summer when I wasn't at church or working, I was mentoring a couple of high school girls. I became really close with Casey, a girl at school who dealt with self-harm as well. She never knew that I had been cutting for years, but I wanted to help her. I guess I thought I was a lost cause. Eventually her parents sent her and her twin sister to a therapeutic boarding school in Kansas City, Missouri.

In July of 2007 I headed off to Palm Beach Atlantic

University. I qualified for their cross-country team and devoted myself to running. I majored in biblical studies and youth ministry, desperately wanting to impact this generation for Christ. I had a great job in the admissions department and felt completely in control of my life. As my pride built, so did my propensity for destruction. I really loved God, but I felt as if He was distant. His presence had waned from my life during this time, and no matter what I did, I could not feel the intimacy I had in the past. I continued restricting and purging, sometimes going days without food. I abused laxatives and ran several times a day.

In October 2007 I was involved in a car accident that totaled my car. This event served as the culmination of every struggle I had faced thus far and forced me to take a serious look at my life. I became depressed and began to separate myself from friends, ministry groups, sports, and everything else I once enjoyed. My grades began to slip. I felt so rejected one night, I cut for the first time in several months. I was utterly desperate. Even though I felt no satisfaction from this act, it seemed to distract me from my pain. I really wanted to die but feared God just enough to stay alive. I thought about death all the time, and by this point I had made two serious attempts to end my life. I quickly realized, along with the help of some mentors, that I needed counseling. I finished my year at Palm Beach Atlantic University and moved back to the Florida Keys. This is when I applied to Mercy Ministries.

I met with a Christian counselor once a week, and after I was living between my mom's house and the woods for a few months, she offered to let me move into her home with her. I got a job across the street that I could ride my bike to. I did well for a while, working and continuing involvement with my church and youth group in the Keys, but I still sensed a chasm between God and me. I was still trying to find my satisfaction in people. After trying to do everything on my own, I finally reached yet another breaking point in November of 2008. That night I wanted to die. I cut far too deep and began to panic. Even though I was losing a lot of blood, I was too full of pride to let anyone know that I had a problem. I wound up walking to the nearby emergency room to have them stitch up my wound. The medical staff then sent me to a psychiatric hospital.

This became another period of clarity for me, and I decided that I didn't want to spend the rest of my life in the isolation room of a treatment center. On March 12, 2009, after a six-month wait, I finally arrived at Mercy Ministries. The transition was rough as my pride battled with submission. I felt like I couldn't trust the staff and constantly rebelled. After some time, however, my heart began to soften, and I began to trust the staff as they continued to work with me.

God began drawing me nearer and nearer as I chose to follow His will and obey the authority in my life. God taught me about the strength in humility, and although humility is still my greatest struggle, I practice being humble every day. I've learned that integrity is an intentional choice, a product of a life submitted to Jesus. My family relationships are being restored as I continue to repair my relationship with my mom.

Our relationship has become a beautiful example of the restoring nature of God.

After graduating from Mercy on September 8, 2009, I was filled with hope, passion, and purpose. I had big dreams, but my biggest would be to someday come back and work for Mercy. I was able to move in with a host family in St. Louis. After a few months I was accepted as a ministry academy intern at the St. Louis Dream Center. I received seminary training and credit hours as well as coordinating children's ministry programs. This experience of real-life ministry opened my eyes to my passion for helping people who were going through some of the same struggles I faced. I made some of my closest friends during this yearlong internship and gained mentors who are still an example in my life today. In December 2010 I was offered a direct-care position at the same therapeutic boarding school that my friend Casey attended two years prior. I moved to Kansas City to work at a school for high-risk teenagers. This Christ-centered ministry allowed me to develop a passion for leadership and discipleship. I developed so much compassion for these teens and the issues they had to work through.

In July of 2011 I was able to go on the first ever Mercy graduate missions trip to Uganda, Africa. We were able to help build classroom facilities and dedicate a home to Watoto Church and their ministry that is raising an orphaned generation in Christ-centered homes and villages. I can't explain what a privilege it was to travel and serve alongside several other Mercy graduates. Even though I'd never met any of these girls, we instantly connected as Mercy sisters, and I felt like I'd known them my whole life. After this trip I could barely stand to be away from Mercy Ministries any longer. I knew that I needed to get involved in some way and asked if I could apply to intern in the Nashville home. They asked me to go ahead and just send in my résumé and apply for a staff position. I was shocked because it was less than two years after I graduated Mercy. I knew that God's promise would come to pass, but I never thought it could happen so soon. Within about a month I was offered a night staff position at Mercy Ministries, Nashville. I was thrilled because the offer came on my two-year anniversary of graduating Mercy. What an amazing testimony of the way God brings lives full-circle! In September 2011 I moved to Nashville to begin my career at Mercy. I worked in the Nashville home for nine months and in June of 2012 I was offered the opportunity to transfer to Mercy St. Louis, the same home I graduated from. I've always felt at home in St. Louis and knew right away that God had opened this door. I am consistently and overwhelmingly blessed by my privilege to work with such a powerful ministry. Every day I look forward to going to work because I get to watch God perform miracles in front of my eyes. I get to sit under leadership filled with the Holy Spirit and marked by wisdom, discernment, and most of all, humility. I get to be a part of something so huge that all I can do is bow down and give God all the glory. My life and countless others have been greatly impacted by Jesus Christ's life-transforming power through Mercy Ministries. I can't imagine a greater call than to serve this vision and mission the rest of my life.

DEBBIE

Growing up, if someone had asked me if I was a Christian, I would have passionately said yes. After all, I attended church every week, sometimes twice a week, I listened to the Bible stories in Sunday school, and I learned how to live as a Christian would. For a long time I did not know the difference between Christ and His church. Church and God were synonymous to me. It wasn't until much later, when I began to experience the world waiting just outside those church doors, that I realized that in all my Christian religiosity, I was missing my own personal relationship with Christ.

At twelve years old I began to wonder if all I had been taught about God had been a lie. During that time I had been befriended by an older man at my local park and was groomed into a full sexual relationship with him. This man was a drug dealer and was ten years my senior. Needless to say, a relationship with drugs, drink, and danger slowly began to replace my relationship with God. After all, if God was my protector, my Father, my Shepherd, then where was He? Why, when I felt at my most vulnerable and most violated, did God not rescue me as He did in all those stories I had listened to and believed when I was a child?

I found myself caught in a downward spiral of helplessness and shame, and my anger burned against a God who I believed had abandoned me, and so I decided that I would abandon Him. I renounced God and vowed to live my life on my own terms. I hit the self-destruct button on my life, and behaviors I thought I was in control of began to escalate and quickly took control of me—self-harm, drug addiction, and sexual addiction. I found myself enslaved to a way of life that was destroying me, and I had given up hope that there was ever a way out.

One day my sister gave me a book called *Mercy Moves Mountains*. There was story after story of girls who were hurting just like me, but they described God in a way I had never known Him. He was real, and as I read, hope began to grow in me. If God had come through for these girls, maybe He would come through for me. A few months later, in February 2001, I was on a plane from Bradford, England, to Nashville, Tennessee, hoping that this place I had read so much about could help me interpret the pain I felt inside, get to the root cause of my rage and rebellion, and introduce me to the God behind the Sunday school stories.

Trust was a big issue for me at Mercy Ministries. I had been hurt by the decisions of other people too many times, and I myself had, in turn, hurt others through my own bad choices and out of my own brokenness. Yet I began to realize that we all have personal choices and that sadly some of us become the victims of other people's bad choices and go on to hurt others. Mercy taught me biblical truths such as forgiveness and my true identity as a daughter of God, and as I applied them to my relationship with Him, I began to understand that I had never been abandoned by Him. As I opened my heart to Jesus, He showed me His heart toward me in those times where I had felt so alone and abused. God did not send the abuse; the Bible teaches that every good and perfect gift comes from God, and abuse is neither of those things. But God did provide a way out of all the effects of abuse, through the power of the cross and redemption. Though there were times I felt separated from Him, I had never been separated from His love for me. The cross of Jesus Christ built a bridge between the Father and me, and with every choice to forgive, to let go, to trust, to speak truth, to stand tall, I took one more step away from the lifestyle that had so destroyed me and into the life He had waiting for me.

After graduating from Mercy Ministries in September 2001, I returned to my hometown in the United Kingdom and enrolled in the Leadership Academy at my church, Abundant Life. One year later I graduated and began working at that same church. During this time I met a godly young man, and we began to date. This relationship was the opposite of everything that I had experienced in the past. It was Christ-centered and pure. We were married within a couple of years with the blessings of both of our families, and we have two children, ages three and one.

Twelve years ago I never imagined that I could have a healthy family, be a wife to my amazing husband, and a mom to my wonderful children. And in my wildest dreams I never once thought that I would be a part of helping bring Mercy Ministries to the UK and eventually become the program director. I am definitely not the same girl who walked through the doors of Mercy Ministries in 2001. I have certainly come full circle because now I get to help other girls overcome many of the same life-controlling issues I once struggled with. I am eternally grateful to be able to share with others the same truths that saved my life.

There is no depth or length He will not go to in order to see the broken restored. Mercy Ministries was certainly a demonstration of that in my life.

MARTHA

I grew up in a Christian family. We went to church every week, and I attended a Christian school from kindergarten through eighth grade. I knew everything about God and Jesus, but the enemy started attacking me at a very early age. When I was two years old, two of my uncles committed suicide just months apart from each other. When I was four, my mom delivered my stillborn sister at full-term. My first memory is holding her in the hospital. Many other family friends passed away too. Before I was ten, I had been to more funerals than I could count. It seemed like death followed me like a shadow. I taught myself to romanticize death so that the sting of it wouldn't hurt as bad. I knew the people who died were Christians and were going to heaven, so I decided that since heaven is better than earth, death must be better than life. This was a lie I believed all the way up until my time at Mercy.

I remember being a very angry child, always yelling at my family, but inside I was just depressed. My parents were more concerned with rules than a relationship, which made it very hard to bond with them like a child normally bonds with his/her parents. I longed for the loving relationship with them that I saw in so many other parent-child relationships, but the emotional connection just wasn't there. My mom and I started seeing a counselor when I was ten, but the original damage was very hard to undo.

At the age of twelve I started cutting myself. I used it as a way to escape from the emotional pain I was feeling. The enemy had also convinced me that I was a bad person and I needed to be punished, so I used it as a way to punish myself. Around the same time that I started cutting, I developed an eating disorder. At the beginning I just used it as a form of control, and it wasn't too serious. But when I entered public high school, body image became very important, and the eating disorder quickly spiraled out of my control. The thing I chose to satisfy my lust for control ended up controlling me.

When I was seventeen and in my senior year of high school, my counselor told me I needed to go to some sort of inpatient treatment. She knew I was a danger to myself because I had become very suicidal. She told me about Mercy Ministries. A few weeks later God miraculously connected me with a graduate from the program. I knew I needed to apply, and I had a lot of support in doing so.

When I applied to the program, my mind-set was one of hopelessness. I didn't think anything would help me, so I thought to myself, "I'll go to this program and I'll do whatever they tell me to, and when it doesn't work, I'll have a good reason to kill myself." I even remember sitting in my counselor's office and telling her, "If this doesn't work, I'm going to kill myself," and she looked straight into my eyes and said,

"OK, Martha." I applied to the program, but during the application process I did attempt suicide and was admitted to the hospital.

The psych ward was a horrible place, and I'm pretty sure I came out of it more suicidal than I was when I went in. Shortly after my hospital stay, on May 20, 2011, I arrived at Mercy. During my time at Mercy God healed me from past scars, freed me from current struggles, and taught me how to live my future. The most important thing I learned at Mercy is that I have a choice. A verse that really spoke to me during my journey was Deuteronomy 30:19 which says, "I have set before you life and death, blessing and curse. Therefore choose life, that you and your offspring may live" (ESV). After hearing this verse quite a number of times before taking it to heart, I chose life!

In the past I was labeled a depressed, suicidal, bulimic, cutter patient, but at Mercy I learned that I am actually a beautiful daughter of the King of the universe. When I chose to believe the truth, it radically changed my life! I realized that I didn't need to punish myself by self-harming because Jesus's blood has already covered all my sins. I learned that I don't need to try to control my outward beauty with an eating disorder because I am fearfully and wonderfully made. This was a hard truth for me accept, but someone told me that calling myself ugly was actually prideful because I was inferring that I could make me better than God did. This made so much sense and helped me learn to see myself as beautiful. I can now look in the mirror and truly see beauty, something I couldn't do before because the eating disorder literally put blinders over my eyes to keep me from seeing it. I forgave people who had hurt me, including myself. I learned to trust God and other people. God spoke to my heart, telling me that He is super trustworthy. I broke agreement with death, which was incredibly freeing! At Mercy I was brought to life and filled with the Holy Spirit. My life was completely transformed. I graduated from Mercy on October 25, 2011.

Since graduating, I have started college, and I'm working toward degrees in accounting and Spanish. I am involved with my church and a campus ministry. God has given me so many opportunities to share His story, my testimony. My relationship with my parents has improved significantly! There is still work to be done, but I love them so much and appreciate all the support they provided during my time at Mercy.

After I graduate college, I plan on either starting or working for a ministry similar to Mercy in a Spanish-speaking country. I have visited Central America several times and have such a love for the people living there. To this day it never ceases to amaze me how many people use the word *joy* to describe me. God literally transformed depression into joy; a desire to die into a passion for life. He used Mercy as the tool to save my life, and I would not be here today without it. I am so thankful that He chose to restore my life and give me hope for my future.

TARA

I was lucky enough not to have any major childhood traumas or anything behind my issues, but it just so happened that my stuff came from the perfect combination of a lot of little factors.

For one thing, I have always been a perfectionist. I was the kid who hated recess because it was so unproductive. From a very early age I put enormous pressure on myself to excel in school and was obsessive about my grades. I'd always been told I was smart and pretty, but I was so self-conscious that I believed I would be totally worthless if I ever lost those qualities.

The only person I knew who loved me unconditionally was my granddad. He was my hero, and I absolutely loved every second we spent together, whether we were doing the Jumble in the Sunday newspaper or dancing around to big band music. When I was in fifth grade, he got extremely sick, and I felt like my whole world was about to collapse. I was so worried that I started restricting my food, but nobody seemed to notice, which made me feel even more worthless.

That summer I went to a vacation Bible school program where I heard about Jesus for the first time, and I said the prayer of salvation. My whole family got saved and started attending the church, and I thought maybe things were about to get better. Unfortunately, a few weeks before Christmas Granddad's health got much worse. On our way to see him in Kansas, a huge snowstorm forced us to pull over, and I knew we weren't going to make it in time. We called Granddad to say good-bye, and I didn't want him to be scared, so I didn't let myself cry, and I kept that tough exterior all through the funeral. I felt like I had to be strong for my family.

After that I went back to acting like the same smiling, friendly girl I had always been, but I kept everything I really felt hidden beneath the surface. I didn't want to let anybody get close because I was afraid I'd either lose them or be rejected. I remember coming home from school almost every day just crying, and restricting my food became my way of coping with bad days.

High school drama made things a lot worse. I was dating this guy at the time who told me I was lucky to have him because he had better options. I eventually broke up with him, and shortly after my dad announced we were moving out of state. I figured I could finally start over, but I was totally alone at my new school and was more stressed out with advanced placement classes than ever before. People started noticing I wasn't as stick-thin as I had been when I was a little kid, which freaked me out beyond all reason. I thought I was starting to lose one of my defining qualities, and I was determined not to let that happen. I never struggled with bingeing, but I started purging to lose whatever weight I could.

Within the year my dad took a higher position with his old company, and I moved back to my old high school. I was really angry at God because I didn't understand why He would bring us to another state only to bring us right back, especially when all the move had done was rip my family apart. There were broken relationships all around me, and I felt I needed to be the savior and heal them.

Obviously that pressure was way too much for anyone to handle, and I felt like a complete failure as a daughter, as a sister, and as a person. I started restricting food excessively and purging even when I wasn't eating just to feel the pain I thought I deserved. Of course I felt horribly guilty throughout all of this because everybody thought I was a "good Christian girl" who volunteered at church and taught Sunday school. I finally told God I didn't want His help and was going to do whatever it took to die from the eating disorder. I lost my appetite almost immediately, so I didn't realize just how close to death I really was.

I graduated from high school in the top of my class and was supposed to go to my dream school that fall, but I was in a complete free fall. I had stopped eating altogether and was purging several times a day. I created elaborate lies to hide my behavior from the people I loved. If there was a time when I couldn't get out of a meal, I would take laxatives that I kept hidden in a Tic Tac box in my purse—anything I could do to keep myself from eating food I didn't think I deserved to eat. I was dizzy, dehydrated, and passing out all the time, but I didn't care.

After forty days of total starvation, just two weeks before school was supposed to start, my body finally gave up. I was literally unable to walk, and my body was rejecting food completely. I had to give up this secret that had been lurking in the shadows of my life for so long, and my family was totally devastated. My parents and doctors admitted me to the hospital immediately, but, you know, me being stubborn, I was still adamant about starting school on time and left the hospital to go to orientation. On the day before classes began, I was exercising a ridiculous amount and blacked out on the stairs outside my dorm room. I was barely conscious, but somehow I managed to call my mom to pick me up. My sister had remembered hearing about a place called Mercy Ministries at a Christian concert several years earlier, and they had me fill out the application on the way back to the treatment center. Just to put this in perspective, the treatment center I was in cost fifteen hundred dollars a day. I figured it out; if Mercy had charged me that much for the time I stayed there, it would have cost me more than $270,000. But Mercy never charged me a dime!

Before going to Mercy, I was in and out of the hospital four more times. I was told my blood sugar was so low most people would have been in a coma or dead, which only made me furious to still be alive! In the program I would halfway listen to the Recovery Night speakers, but I was always so frustrated to hear them say they still had eating-disordered thoughts 40 percent of the day. That seemed pointless to me—I wanted 100 percent freedom or death, and at that point death seemed more likely. To make matters worse, my doctors told me total freedom was possible for some people but certainly not for me. A psychiatrist told me she expected to be speaking at my funeral in the near future, and I believed her.

I know a lot of you have probably heard similar things from people on your treatment team because they're trying to scare you into realizing how serious this is. And if you have, I just want you to know that yes, this is absolutely serious, but I know God has an amazing plan for each of your lives, just like He had other plans for me. It's absolutely critical to have a treatment team that believes in your future too.

The one person on my treatment team who always believed in me was my spectacular dietitian, Lindsay. I first met her when she was working at the hospital, and I started seeing her outpatient once I left the program. I know I would never have been able to keep myself medically stable enough to get into Mercy without her help. I would come to her week after week still *not* following the meal plan we had agreed on, but she would always point out the things I was getting better at and tell me she knew some day we'd be able to go out to lunch for fun without me having a complete nervous breakdown. Of course I told her there was no way that would ever happen back then, but she seemed so confident that I wanted to believe her, although I'm sure she had her doubts about me too!

Thankfully I was accepted to Mercy on May 15, 2008. I arrived at the home in St. Louis absolutely terrified. I had never expected to live long enough to make it into the program, which was the main reason I had even agreed to apply in the first place. But deep inside me I had a tiny speck of hope that maybe all my doctors were wrong, maybe things could actually change. I never would have admitted it back then, and the hope seemed to come and go with my moods anyway. For a while I used all the same techniques I had used to push people away in the past. At first I tried telling the staff that I believed God had just called me there to scare me so I wouldn't go back to what I had been doing before. I was fine; I didn't need any help. That wasn't very convincing, so I went back to being rebellious and trying to get kicked out. Just like we've all heard before, the behaviors I was using to protect the eating disorder were caused by deeper issues, and at Mercy you actually have the time to figure out what those issues are and how to deal with them.

All the girls have counseling once a week, and after I got over my initial phase of freezing my counselor out and refusing to talk (that took about a month), we started to talk about my thoughts about God and my relationship with Him. This really irritated me at first because I was so used to thinking of the eating disorder as my biggest problem in life. Honestly that's the thing that makes Mercy so different. I remember at the other treatment centers they had me try to replace my thoughts with affirmations. For example, your negative thought is, "I'm ugly," so your affirmation is, "I'm beautiful." I think this is the right idea, but it never changed anything for me because something was missing. I had nothing to base that new affirmation on. I could look in the mirror for an hour straight and tell myself I was beautiful, but I could "see" with my distorted eyes that it just wasn't true.

At Mercy the reason they focus on your relationship with God so much in the beginning is that you need somebody to trust. That way when you start trying to change these destructive thought patterns, you go to the Bible and see what God says. For example, my original thought was, "I'm ugly." I went to the Bible and found verses such as Ecclesiastes 3:11, "God has made everything beautiful for its own time. He has planted eternity in the human heart, but even so, people cannot see the whole scope of God's work from beginning to end" (NLT). Then I could say,

"This is my time, and God has made me beautiful for it," and I was actually able to believe it because it wasn't coming from me. It was coming from God, and I knew I could believe what He said.

I wish I had time to tell you every step of my journey through Mercy, but let me just say that it was an incredibly slow, slow process. I was in the program with girls who had totally different experiences where they just came in and were super motivated and just had a blast going through Mercy. That definitely wasn't the case with me, but I wouldn't change one second of my time there, so don't feel like your journey to freedom has to be the same as anybody else's. For me it felt like I was trying to tear down a brick wall...one brick at a time! I had always known that "God so loved the world," but once I started learning how much God loved me personally, exactly as I was, everything else *slowly* began to fall away.

I realized I never had to be the savior for my family; God pretty much had that under control and didn't need my help! It was one of the most difficult, painful processes I've ever gone through, but I'm so glad God gave me the strength to stay with it.

I graduated from the program on November 18, 2008, and my life has been absolutely crazy and wonderful since. It was scary at first to deal with situations without going back to my old coping habits, but I knew this time I had the tools to fight away the negative thoughts that used to consume my every moment. I just finished my senior year at Belmont University in Nashville, where I studied journalism and public relations. I am officially a college graduate! This summer I'll be interning at the largest public relations firm in Tennessee, and I hope to eventually work for a nonprofit organization—maybe even Mercy! For the past year I've been dating an incredible guy who loves God and loves me unconditionally. He's been so wonderfully supportive of my time at Mercy, and he's exactly the kind of man all my Mercy sisters and I used to dream about finding someday. I can't even begin to tell you how amazing it feels not to be chained to scales and calories any more.

But the best part of finding freedom has been watching the ripple effect on the lives of others. My extended family has always been very secretive, but since my time at Mercy several of my cousins have opened up and sought help for their own issues with alcoholism and depression. I've also had the chance to meet several girls who applied to Mercy because the dietitian at my old treatment center told them that if Mercy could help me, they could help anybody! At Mercy they teach you that your healing is not just for you, and now I have seen that principle play out in my life.

And that goes for all of you too. There are people on the other side of all the awful things you're going through now, and they are the ones who need you to show them that they're worth it too. So that's why you have to make up your mind that you're going to fight for your freedom with everything you have. No matter what you've done or what's been done to you or how many times you've been in treatment, *you are never ever beyond hope*. I remember my first week at Mercy. I would just lie in bed and cry myself to sleep because I wanted to give up, and my roommate was getting ready to graduate, so she drilled this verse into my head to encourage me every night. It's a scripture verse, and I think *The Message* translation is the best; it says: "Stay with it—that's what is required. Stay with it to the end. You won't be sorry; you'll be saved!" (Mark 13:13).

SUZANNE

As an outsider looking in, no one ever guessed the turmoil that I lived in every day. The abuse I experienced as a child was to me "normal." I lived a very sheltered life and as a result did not have any healthy relationships with adults that I felt I could confide my secrets with.

My family was constantly changing churches, and at a young age I developed the belief that I was "predestined *not* to be a child of a God." At the age of thirteen, after suffering once again at the hands of my abuser, I lost all will to live and drank fingernail polish remover, fully expecting not to wake up in the morning. Yet by God's mercy I did wake up, though I saw it as a curse and not a blessing. I couldn't die and had no idea how to live. As a result, I fell into a life of silence and was known as the quiet, good girl. No one knew I was screaming inside.

I eventually left home for college where I pursued a degree in deaf education. My silence slowly began to break, as I was able to express myself through sign language. At the same time I became involved in a campus ministry where I heard for the first time that God truly loved me and had not rejected me. Hungry for truth, I fell in love with this God who loved and accepted me.

My new friends encouraged me to get involved in a local church, yet because of my past I declined over and over again until one friend suggested that I serve at a homeless dinner and attend the Bible study afterward. For me this was a perfect compromise. Through serving at the dinner, God began to light a passion in me for the inner city. I began attending church regularly, and six months later with two of my friends I moved into the inner-city neighborhood where my church was located.

I graduated from college and began pursuing my dream of teaching and interpreting. My past still haunted me, but I pushed it aside, assuming that this is what Christians do.

After three years of living and working in the inner city, my world came crashing down. I was gang raped. I had been carpooling to my new teaching job with one of my co-teachers. After a month of carpooling, one day on the way back home my coworker turned off the normal route and delivered me to four men who took turns repeatedly raping me. When it was over, my co-teacher brought me back home and drove off.

Falling back into a life of silence, I coped the only way I knew how, and that was to not say anything. I began to be tortured by memories of my past as well as what had happened recently. I lived with the secret of what had happened for months before I confided in my best friend. It became clear to me and my friend that I could not continue to minister to the youth in the neighborhood when I was so broken myself. My friend suggested that I apply to Mercy Ministries. (We had books in our home to reference for the young ladies in the neighborhood. Never in a million years did I actually think that God had planted those books in my home for me.) Mercy provided a safe haven for my healing, addressing lies that I didn't realize I still believed about God, authority, and myself. At Mercy I was given the space and love to help me find my voice again. One thing that I will always remember is when the staff would say, "You never know who is on the other side of your healing." Yet, for me, I did know some of the faces of the youth in my neighborhood who were waiting for me on the other side.

I graduated from Mercy in June 2007 knowing in my heart I was being called back to the inner city. It was a definite transition back; there were many fears, but at Mercy I had been given the tools to fight the lies and the fears that tried to steal my joy.

In the summer of 2008 I was approached by one of the pastors at my church and asked if I would consider being the director of the tutoring and dance program and help develop a nonprofit in the neighborhood where I lived. With great excitement I accepted. Mercy taught me how to stand on the truth and what it means to trust God even when life is not making sense. I face heartache every day at my job; I hold broken children every week and have the privilege of pointing them to Jesus and showing them a different way. Because Mercy was there in my darkest hour, I am now free and living out my freedom among others that they may see God's love and invite Him to heal their young hearts as well.

Notes

CHAPTER SEVEN
THE THIRD OPTION

1. "Jesus Loves Me" by Anna Bartlett Warner. Public domain.

CHAPTER EIGHT
HEART OF THE MATTER

1. Courtney Hutchison, "Self-Harm Videos on YouTube: Dangerous or Therapeutic?", ABC News, http://abcnews.go.com/Health/WomensHealth/harm-vids-youtube-dangerous-therapeutic/story?id=12950980 (accessed March 15, 2013).

2. Walden Behavioral Care, "Eating Disorder Affects 1 in 5 Young Women," http://www.waldenbehavioralcare.com/eating-disorder-affects-1-in-5-young-women/ (accessed March 15, 2013).

January 2013 marks thirty years since the desire God put in my heart became a reality called Mercy Ministries. I thought I was starting one home for troubled young women. I had no idea this would grow to become multiple homes in America, as well as homes in other nations.

—Nancy Alcorn
Founder of Mercy Ministries

Homes in the United States:
Monroe, Louisiana
Nashville, Tennessee
St. Louis, Missouri
Sacramento, California

International Affiliates:
Bradford, United Kingdom
Auckland, New Zealand
Vancouver, BC, Canada

Monroe, Louisiana: Opened 1983

Nashville, Tennessee: Opened 1996

International Headquarters, Nashville, Tennessee: Opened 2001

St. Louis, Missouri: Opened 2005

Sacramento, California: Opened 2009

Bradford, United Kingdom: Opened 2006

Auckland, New Zealand: Opened 2007

Vancouver, BC, Canada: Opened 2010

If you are a young woman who is hopeless, desperate, and hurting, I am telling you today that there is an answer! Freedom and restoration are possible…freedom from tough issues such as sexual abuse, eating disorders, cutting, addictions, unplanned pregnancy, sex trafficking, and more. No matter what the problem is, Jesus Christ is the answer!

And Mercy Ministries can help. If you are struggling, please visit www.MercyMinistries.com and apply to our program.

Also, if you know of a girl who is struggling with any of these issues and needs a time of intensive discipleship in a residential setting, please don't hesitate to contact Mercy Ministries. We would like to help her! There is no problem too big for God.

Perhaps God is calling you to get involved with the work we do. I pray that you will answer that call and take part in this work of restoration. God's doing amazing things here at Mercy, and we need faithful supporters in order to continue what we are doing and to expand this ministry.

If you want to be actively involved, please see the following page for more information. Together we can make a great difference.

Nancy Alcorn

"For I know the plans I have for you," declares the L ORD, *"plans to **prosper** you and not to harm you, plans to give you **hope and a future**."* —Jeremiah 29:11

Check out our **website, www.MercyMinistries.com,** to find out more information about Mercy Ministries regarding the following:

- How to become a financial donor
- To obtain an application for admission
- For national and international locations of Mercy Ministries' homes
- To receive information about our adoption services
- To receive updates about Mercy Ministries and the work we are doing
- To purchase product resources

Mercy Ministries asks that you please contact our international headquarters in Nashville, Tennessee, for additional information regarding the following:

- Speaking engagements
- Employment opportunities
- Volunteer opportunities
- All other inquiries

Mercy Ministries of America
P.O. Box 111060
Nashville, TN 37222-1060
Phone: 615.831.6987
Fax: 615.315.9749
Email: info@mercyministries.com
Website: www.MercyMinistries.com

ABOUT THE AUTHOR

Nancy Alcorn spent the first eight years of her career working for the state of Tennessee. Her time with the government included five years with the Department of Corrections working with juvenile delinquent girls, and three years with the Department of Human Services working in Emergency Protective Services investigating child abuse cases and supervising foster care.

It was during this time of government work that Nancy realized the inadequacy of these programs to offer real transformation in the lives of troubled individuals. Out of this experience came a driving passion for broken young girls that led to the birth of Mercy Ministries in 1983. Since that time, numerous residential and outreach programs have been established in various locations across America and other nations around the world. The ministry continues to grow and expand.

Nancy frequently speaks at conferences around the world, and in 2012 she was appointed to the Evangelical Council for Financial Accountability's Board of Reference, where she joined other prominent members such as Franklin Graham as an ambassador for financial accountability in leading Christian nonprofit organizations. She resides in Nashville, which is also the home of the international headquarters of Mercy Ministries.

ABOUT MERCY MINISTRIES

Since 1983 Mercy Ministries' free-of-charge, voluntary Christian residential program has served a diverse population of young women ages 13–28 who have been physically and sexually abused, including victims of sex trafficking, as well as those who face life-controlling issues such as eating disorders, self-harm, drug and alcohol addictions, depression, and unplanned pregnancy. Mercy Ministries of America serves hurting young women from across the United States and has residential homes in Monroe, Louisiana; Nashville, Tennessee; St. Louis, Missouri; and Sacramento, California. We also have three international locations in the United Kingdom, Canada, and New Zealand.

VISION STATEMENT
Mercy Ministries is committed to being an effective and well-respected global organization dedicated to transforming lives of generations searching for truth and wholeness.

MISSION STATEMENT
Mercy Ministries exists to provide opportunities for young women to experience God's unconditional love, forgiveness, and life-transforming power.

GUIDING PRINCIPLES
- Take girls in free of charge
- Tithe 10 percent to other ministries
- Never accept money with strings attached or that would inhibit our ability to share biblical truths with the girls

For more information on Mercy Ministries and its global affiliates, **please visit www.MercyMinistries.com.**

For constant updates, follow us on social media!

 FIND US ON FACEBOOK:
facebook.com/MercyMin
facebook.com/NancyAlcorn

 FIND US ON TWITTER:
twitter.com/MercyMinistries
twitter.com/NancyAlcorn

 FIND US ON BLOGSPOT:
NancyAlcorn.com

 FIND US ON PINTEREST:
pinterest.com/MercyMinistries

 LISTEN TO OUR PODCAST:
www.MercyTalk.org

Mercy Ministries of America
P.O. Box 111060
Nashville, TN 37222
Phone: 615.831.6987